This is the first print version
of the creative writing journal,
Route 57, and its eleventh issue:
a fuller version is available at
www.route57.group.shef.ac.uk.
We are proud of the work the
students at the University
of Sheffield have produced over
the years, and are particularly
pleased to be able to showcase
that work in physical book
form: it materializes the virtual
excellence of the creative writing
and allows the book to wander
into the world, especially into
the crannies, nooks, book shelves
and bookshops of the city.

The title of this volume, as some
of you might have guessed, is
an anagram of Route Fifty-Seven
(and preferred to 'Everyone
Stuff It', also an anagram of the
same words) — and I hope
you'll enjoy the feisty font revue
designed so splendidly by

Route 57
#11

Sevi Landolt and Manu Meyer of
'Go! Grafik'. The publication
and Arts Enterprise funding would
not have happened without
the ever inventive and imaginative
Matthew Cheeseman.

I would also like to thank all the
staff and student editors who
worked so hard to edit the many
contributions received, and to
present such great work to deadline.
Route 57 has been going since
2006 so celebrates its ninth
anniversary this year. It has always
sought to publish in all five genres,
poetry, fiction, drama, non-fiction
and experimental writing, and
a selection from all is presented in
this volume. Most of all, it works
because of the creativity and
imaginative daring of the students
at the University of Sheffield.
Enjoy!

Adam Piette,
General Editor, Route 57

Authors

Poetry

Angelina Ayers
Chad Bentley
Ryan Bramley
Joe Caldwell
Oliver Clark
John Darley
Beth Davyson
Jenny Donnison
Benjamin Dorey
Georgia Elander
Veronica Fibisan
Anna Fojtel
Georgia Haggar
Lucy Holt
Gary Hughes
Aidan Jenner
Sam Kendall
Joshua Lingard
William Lloyd
Martin Malone
Alex Marsh
Catriona McLean
Amber McNamara
Bridie Moore
Helen Mort
Colombine Neal
Mattias Ostblom
Ellie Pearce
Karl Riordan
Katie Smart
Lucy Smith
Nathan Spencer

David J Troupes
Anastasia Van Spyk
Joe Vaughan
Sam Wadkin
William Watts
Matilda Webb
Mark Wood

Experimental

Timothy Plant

Non-Fiction

Camille Brouard
Emily Reed
Rebecca Solomon
Jack Stacey
William Watts

Drama

Greg Challis

Fiction

Val Derbyshire
Peter S Dorey
Nick Gore
Alex Marsh
Catriona McLean
Catherine Stanford
Hannah White

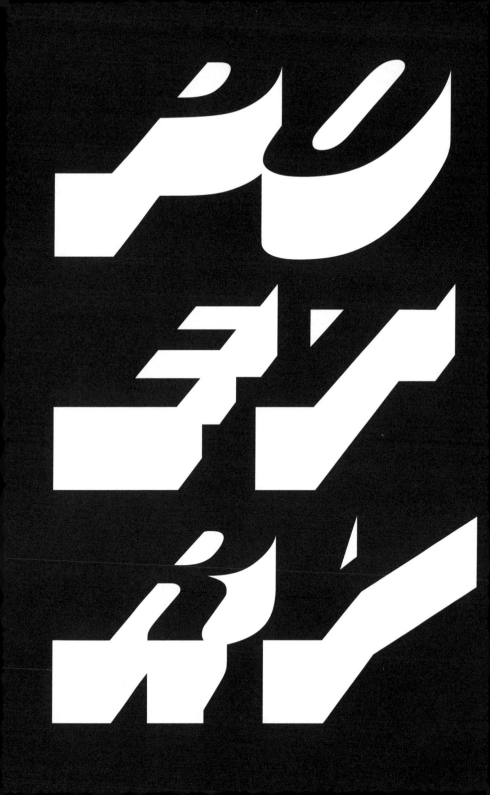

Editors

Ágnes Lehóczky
John Darley
Jenny Donnison
Vera Fibisan
Joshua Lingard
Alex Marsh
Catriona McLean
Colombine Neal
Joe Vaughan
William Watts

Crush

Obsess is an ugly word, she says, in the beige
and paper atrophy of 19th Century Fiction.
Marching drums are just turning off Arundel,
slogans blowing in the late May wind

while she flicks between pages of Bronte
and the stairwell, where any minute he might emerge.
I admire her ability to blush, instinctive
as an animal ready to run at the whiff of fox.

                    My skin is inexpressive.
I've heard this makes me hard to read.

  *

Not obsessed, then. But to bear one thought
into every room — imagine the thought is a moth
precarious on her thumb-nail, wings folded
like pages, no less absurd than when it first settled
harmless as rain.
                She's fond of the moth,
weighs her movements against the risk of flight,
wrist braced at an angle to lock them eye
to compound eye. Now what if he does emerge
from the stairwell, rushes across the room
to touch her frozen fingers —

will she reciprocate, take his hand
                and send the moth fluttering?

  *

Those marching drums, the clarinetists
with their band camps, their arpeggios, always
a bagatelle to perfect, and no time
between metronome beats for this ill-lit desire
              to what — converse, coexist?

Tomorrow, I'll join the orchestra,
learn cor anglais to fill my head with noise.
I want to be someone else's delusion,
turn tail on their meaningful looks,
              walk home alone

      through low cloud and snickets
thick in morning glory to practice my scales.

Angelina Ayers

Six shoulders

We carried the tank inside the church
an invading force on six shoulders.
Step. Stop. Step. Stop.
A marching rhythm hindered by mud,
between pews dug in like trenches,
lined with sand-bags and mouldy wood,
lined with bibles and hymn books frayed with time.
Here prayers are spoken for prayers sake
under the watchful eyes of a needy god.
There prayers are spoken for the end in sight
under the watchful eyes of a
machine gun turret set up in the pulpit.

Young men can die outside of wartime;
just in single figures rather than in single file.
Those who go together en masse are remembered
by a polished plaque, but those who shuffle
off alone adorn only mantle pieces at home.
Is it better to fall in a foreign humour tinged with bullets,
or tinged with tumours in foreign halls?

Step. Stop. Step. Stop.
An invading force on six shoulders
we carried the tank inside the church.
It was much easier to lift when broken.

Chad Bentley

縁 (`En`)

Fate. A thing I once mocked when intoxicated
with island whisky and thoughts of long ago.
There was no reason to it. No need
to bother myself with method, motive, reason.
There is no god, no other. Just ourselves
to blame for the cause of our misfortunes.

There you stood. A miracle
not even you could explain. The things you saw,
the things that were, now etched upon your mind,
a procession of perplexities
            only you could fathom.

        You thank the scars
        for bringing you here.

When I took in the words that were
            your story,
my ears burned. I closed my eyes,
tried to understand the lines, the tones.
How they danced around my head,
until correlations of colour
            struck me
                        with fear.
Once I had seen them,
I could not make them
                        go away.

My Fukushima became a nightmare.
amidst their faces and their screams,
the debris and the ghostly radiation,
stood there silently
            in the middle of it all
was you.

Your Fukushima was home.
Your composition, a requiem for home.
Your lyrical refrain was brought to our ears
by a beautifully strange coincidence.
Fate. A thing I once mocked when intoxicated.
We sat in the Red Deer, glass in hand,
Sobered by your words.

Ryan Bramley

Arrival

The city from the train
is cobalt, chrome and cotton wool,
softened to a painting
by hangover and morning mist.

In the sunshine the station
is clean and welcoming as
eiderdown,
but my legs move smoothly,
with purpose, and my stomach
lurches

as the taxi stutters
into second and away
along the black ribbon of road
to where she's waiting.

Joe Caldwell

in the middle of nowhere

a plane slips through the coded stars
winking at my complicity
in our relative, certain proximity

Oliver Clark

choke

a voice breaks
the silence; echoes, mocking.
i hold my breath
until its gone

Oliver Clark

yesterday, it was summer

my skin prickled warm
yesterday, it was summer
and i never knew
the rain is so cold

Oliver Clark

Siebenschläfer

'And when they had taken their refection and sat in weeping and
wailings, suddenly, as God would, they slept.'
The Golden Legend — The story of the seven sleepers

Each moment dips into the next
like overlapping silhouettes.
They breathe while they sleep,
and sleep while they breathe.
Hibernating religious refugees
dream of fire-flickering shadows
scattered across the cave's dimpled epidermis.

Buried in forgotten gliraria,
seven steady rhythms rumble;
stone lungs echo with distant voices.
Eyes torn from walls are touched by
shattering light.
A three hundred year breath yawns from
its body-warmed cave.

'The Dormouse slowly opened his eyes. "I wasn't asleep," he said in a
hoarse, feeble voice: "I heard every word you fellows were saying."'
Alice's Adventures in Wonderland

John Darley

Metronome

They, the metronome
  ache with the threat of cold lust —
  move like a cracked mirror.
They, the metronome
  with naked leg and split spine
  convulse like surging fluid.
They, the metronome
  who breathe creosote air
  bite with iron, acid and tooth.
They, the metronome
  born as ghosts,
  from the residue of rapture:
a tick
and a kick,
 and the regular
  click of wheels on rails;
   a timeless tempo
        of twisted metal
           into
             tamed skull.
     Trepanned
       until the ticking stops.
     A muted march from
          mother
       to
         incinerator.
           Each moment
              weighed like a
              fat egg.
           Each moment
         pulled down
             the throat until
          each moment
       touches the next.
    A wreck
      that will not rest,
 remains in a lucid dream,
      animated
by the metronome's fingers.

A loss of blood somewhere.
A slow leak only heard at night.
Siphoned away to this quiet mirage.

John Darley

A Priori

'In spite of the fact that science could produce enormous horror in
the world, it is of value because it can produce *something*.'
The Pleasure of Finding Things Out Richard Feynman

'Make the bomb work'
was spoken like we were
jump-starting God.
Rattled away on empty trains
and buried into the desert's husk
like ticks amongst rock and dust.
Gathered together to whittle
a fist-full of stuff
into something more simple.

I picked locks for fun,
scratched around
and danced in moon-lit sand;
I tuned human computers that bustled
with the grey smell of plastic and chalk.

An idea lurched from the desert
fresh-faced and eager-mouthed.
We knocked a man over from two miles away.
We burned the sand into glass with our new fire.

A necessary conception unspooled
across the desert like a detonation wire.
A key that opened two locks:
one to heaven, and one to hell.
A moment that caught in the throat
when discovery became invasion.

When we dropped the bomb on Hiroshima,
we danced in Los Alamos.

Here, squat blocks grown under thrusting pylons,
ceaseless construction rattles through Central Park's twisted leaves.
The heaving building rises
from grey mud and, like a Nephilim,
its complacent figure towers over the city.

I conjure the hot dry memory,
it ignites above 35th street.
I watch the little star expand
across the sky, pushing down,
evaporating heavy buildings.
My coffee cup, raised to my lips as
the shockwave arrives at the park
and pulls everything away.
After the blast,
no wind, and no blood; only
that electrical smell of iron and teeth.

The Nephilim continues its rattle.
And coffee remains streaming.
Behind me, a clash of clumsy crockery:
a single white plate scuttles past my legs.
Its escape slows to a gentle spin,
the edge wobbling on the pavement.

Imagine a point on the plate's edge
tracing a single curving line,
drawn around itself.
Imagine billions of them,
rushing into my mouth and lungs;
immaculate points dissolving against eager optic nerves.
This is worth it.

John Darley

Lines

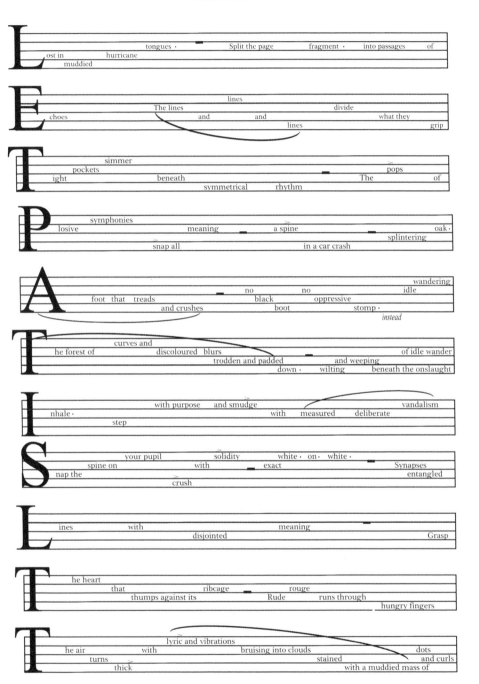

P
heart
ounding   bulges and   Seams of   strands   strain   through
splits   curled

O
ne   fist ·
and   many   of white   to a   through heavy
nothing   squeeze   sharp white noise

R
ed·   chest   lines until
red ·   as the heart   in its open   red   through the
red ·   blackens   gasping

E
outside   heat   in the air
like an   hall   all red   hanging   grasping at cooling ash
mpty   empty

John Darley

Helping hand

I seek a friend in the process
lose some skin from my face
do not
   pacify me
I know
      better than this yet
today will give nothing more
            I'm glad
to ignore you
spend time
in parks unpeacefully or watching
           over
negotiations of pigeons
             brittle skinned what's amazing
is how I am willing
never to spend another day
     in this rooftop locker

Beth Davyson

Let me assure you

I've tried
Don't doubt it I took the bark from the one tree
     worth drawing it was a tree
that might have fallen had I not
 stopped

I rubbed the bark on my teeth am yet
to notice the difference

Back where I live
I knocked
     thought of that weak voice as a request
for absence
   I sucked in as though someone were proud
of my ability to breathe poorly

wondered if disappearance might
   be worth another shot
         if not now
perhaps tomorrow

Beth Davyson

Hair removal

Do you remember
    a dog bit your face
your mother denies nothing

I do not wish to bring this up
only you talk as though
      perhaps you know

lines beyond these down hairs
    in our moustache areas
christ
    is it really our fault
we have breasts
  we wake up wishing to be pregnant so we
might complain at sickness

and is it really normal
  pink smeared on smile
ripped off, that
        our mouths recover from all things

Beth Davyson

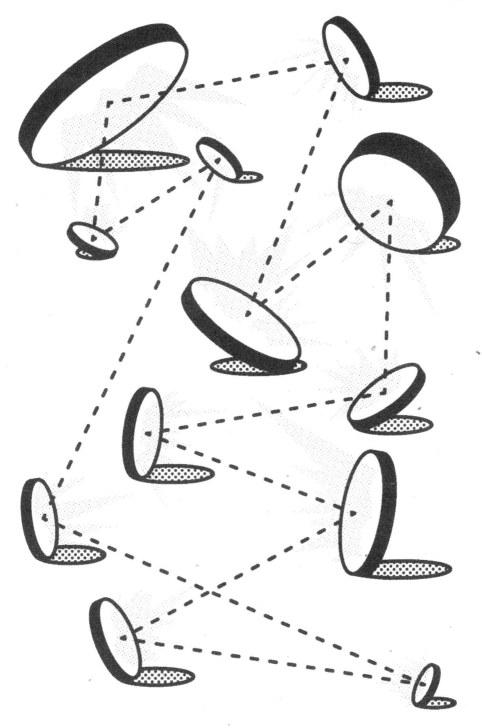

The pollinators of Maoxian, Sìchuān Province, China

When the ruler wants a plank, his ministers cut down a tree,
When the ruler wants a fish, his ministers dry up a valley.
    Huainanzi 淮南子 (second century BC).[1]

The pear and apple orchards blossom.
Diligent pollinators move

among the slender boughs,
their fine brushes dipped in harvested pollen

from earlier blooms, a mix of pistils, stamens,
dusty yellow grains.

Delicately they stroke each flower,
the process painstaking, an art

that human hands now master,
thousands labouring so trees may bear fruit.

Spring orchards are silent. Breezes shiver branches
but air no longer

hums and buzzes. Gone the whirr of wings;
butterflies, bees, all the insects

eradicated, a triumph of efficiency.
Cameras capture

happy farmers perched in trees in drifts of flowers.
Here a smiling girl

her national dress carnelian red,
richly embroidered, her cap

a shade of azure. Her timeless pose implies
it was always this way.

Jenny Donnison

1 My thanks to Professor Roel Sterckx of Cambridge University for supplying this quote.

At Rouen, 1916,
in memory of my grandfather

Close to forty, ox-strong.
Pictured in white at the gymnasium,
palms clouded in chalk,
balanced one-handed on a pommel horse,
and here, suspended from still rings,
mouth set stubborn.

No faded photographs in khaki.
You said you would not kill
so they sent you to Rouen
unloading barges of coal.

When you were insubordinate
they tied you to a tree,
arms outstretched in the pouring rain.
Cut you down half-dead at dusk.

After, you rarely spoke of it.
Told only of green and tender buds,
the miraculous spring.

Jenny Donnison

Halcyon

It can't be that only the righteous see them.
We count six strung out on a twelve mile stretch.
Each orange–blue lucifer
sparks the trout brown river, the dipping trees.
They weave invisible skeins
from bank to bank,
mark their domain with piping calls.

Barely bigger than a sparrow,
squat with outsized head, a spear of beak.
Once hung by a thread to foretell the weather
or used by fishermen in feathery lures.

Each feather alone is dull.
Brilliance flares
as light plays on the living whole.

Jenny Donnison

Urban fox

sky's eyelid is shut
I scavenge pickings of light
pinpricks and thin shine
torn in the world's tarp

swift lope over glitter cold clods
wriggle through hedge roots to hard black
white startle
metallic animal roars past
trails miasma of burn

brisk trot along grass path
ignore swoop of flat-faced owl
out back all quiet
nose through heady stink
mould and rot
bread and fruit
manna of fried chicken
parcelled in plastic
carry home to den

Jenny Donnison

Blur

> 'I passed beyond the unreality of the thing
> represented, I entered crazily into the spectacle, into
> the image, taking into my arms what is dead'
> Roland Barthes, *Camera Lucida*

After communion, some sunday lunch,
the garden.
Three generations line up
bucket smiles for us.
There's me at the end—
lips flared in acceptance that
memory is sometimes shared.

White knuckles crack
against the net of the lens.
Pupils make irises
shrink in the shade,
sink in a face made cherubic
by pale skin glowing with
overexposure; sulphur burns
blur its edges.

Translucent waif — chased
from childrens' wards to the Word.
Wrapped by my Grandfather's arm
and the sandalwood scent of his robes.
His mountains and ministry hang
love and truth on a small stretched chest.

Keen as my newly needed razor,
flowers wilt at feet washed
by storms of serotonin
misfiring all spring
until the garden — the world —
reeks of almonds and wounds.

Now flatline lips flicker
as a grasshopper mimics a camera's click.
Then they twitch: That's it! Or maybe. It was.

Benjamin Dorey

Cold War

He appears each evening by my desk, as
outside dusk dissolves into starlight.
His right shoulder — my left — grows opaque
in the glass and the soft light of paper lampshades.

He glares each morning, and sometimes at night:
as I brush my teeth from left to right
he brushes right to left, spitting blood
from the same thin gums.

Between the shower specked window and
a dirty mirror, he shrinks into infinity
until caught in a raindrop—
sinking out of view, then reappearing—

trapped in the ice of the window pane.
His eyes dilate into inky marbles
and his grins curl to snarls
even as I force out smiles.

He's still there when I pull the rusty curtains,
flicking the switch to pitch us into darkness.
I still keep the knife beside the pills
and jolt awake when killing him in dreams.

Benjamin Dorey

"   "

It sits nestled snugly between the sixty six and the ninety nine, mocks the roundness of one hundred, spurts into life borne on every last gasp and death rattle. A baby clutching cot bars sends smiles or sometimes wails at its absence/presence. It hangs behind each present and each punch, invested in every ululating note of sex and singing, in the hollow bowls of stadiums brimming with the thick air of voices. It stalks the edges of picture frames, hovering between the whitewashed walls and loud floors of galleries, haunts the poem from the right of the page, bears the blue ghosts of cigarette smoke skywards from beer gardens glowing like ships, borne on the navy ocean of moors under moonlight. It blooms behind the closed eyes of the communion rail, wraps the prayer wheels of temples with the holiest mantras — it is holier and more holey than the holy — resting best in the blindness of desert caves. It prowls the freezing waters of the furthest fathoms, the saucer eyes of creatures in the deep, is raised to the sky by sunlight kissing the white tips of waves, then pours from clouds as they stroke the hillsides. What is it is what it is, resonating the world in and out of existence for us, strange abscess in the tissue of   everything we are.

Benjamin Dorey

Candlestick

A year later, you were still tracing the sequence in your sleep:
Five foot from the floor,
Left leg bent neatly over bar, point toes
With as much grace as you can muster;
Right leg wound into the rope, once, twice,
Foot flexed hard into the thick hard twine;
Then breathe deep, let go your blistered palms' sticky, sweaty grip
And droop backwards, slowly,
Til your fingers meet the surface of the rubber bed below,
Your body suspended,
Spine arched,
Torso stretched taut.

Back then you loved your body
For what it could do:
Fold forward at the waist to bow
Over legs butterflied wide;
Or roll eleven cartwheels in a row,
Legs and arms rigid, braced
Against earth, now air,
And again,
Like a messy, wheeling star.

Georgia Elander

Plenty

On the apex of the spread
of tidal pools   your hair
sea anemone on the skin
of a rock   dry-swept
by coastal winds.

Gather in naphtha flare clouds
around the balloon,
softened by landscape
the waves boil over each rock,
myriads of barnacles and mussels
open maps to treasures
while velvet crabs scuttle
trailing sand veils.

Limpets cling together,
their underside orange,
sinks behind the waterwall,
my finger buds
a caress,
the waves have reached high rock
and threaten,
anemone winnows hands
with water.

Veronica Fibisan

Crevice

Pinned on the geological table
at the edge where pellucid water
scatters and churns
infant fingers of rock,
timorous walled corklets
retreat into navels
some green, some bleeding.

In-between folds of coralline skin
swept by sand rushes,
you hide your new found strength
subtle grip as you wait for Andromeda,
discard cowry shells
here and there, ashore,
shriveled algae coats pebble toes,
limpet nails,
buried in the sand
among the detritus
of your once full womb.

Veronica Fibisan

Barnacle

today it was the moonless night
the tide retreats into its shell
reveals hollows and summits
on this waveworn body
I divide memories into recyclable
unrecyclable
debris collected from reflux time lapses
succoured to this oyster stuck to rock
pairs of fringed fingers comb the ripples
blink scuttal valves close
domular shaped shadows
reel in ring lines from edge water
cast away hands back to myself

Veronica Fibisan

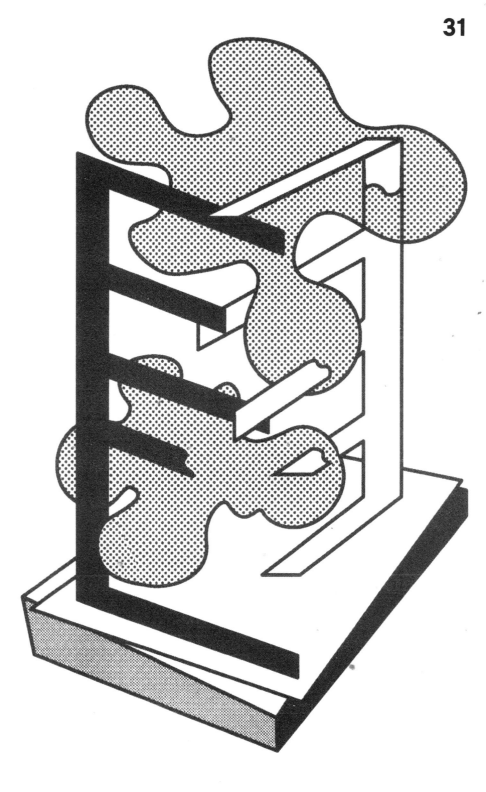

Pepper

No more space in the ground
to bury the corpses. For corpses
spread like mushrooms after the rain;
the chimney bids them farewell:

the unconfined,
                          pepper

settles on our lips, spoils the flavour
of soups and warm bread
or sinks into the roots in fields.
Flowers may whisper their epitaph;
The flowers that grow
on the boosted pastures and grass.

The sky's lungs are full,
                          about to choke.

Never mind the rain.

Anna Fojtel

The Great Silence, or a great silence

Blue, deep depth of the profound bottle neck,
emptiness that is sublime in complication. Simplicity
swelling amongst forever's murk. A flash of life in the
death of it all when this light precedes from, where? When
existence was designed it was intentional, or perhaps
the hypothesis of the fateful encounter? Maybe. Unlikely in the
heat of the dark that this cold should be all there is. Not a murmur
or a whisper comes creeping past Andromeda, her hush
secludes the Titans. On a plane of existence, there is nothing
that exists beyond, outside a recess. To survive in the deep
is to remain a fossil, to ignore the flourish in the heights. But
to accept is unacceptable, to create a paradox is to live. In a
strive for the absolute, in the bitterness, an absolution. It is
our beauty to never achieve, to invent the profound, and
to die in its search. Such a divine act of futility, to give up
remains a warning. Carry on no further in this unending game, a
charade to eliminate. Allow the silence, let it prevail and
in deafness triumph.

Georgia Haggar

Intermission

You've not been paying much attention
to the hedges around your head.
They are fizzing like drawings and pressed for time.

Which scab have you been picking at today?
No one's seen you eat. Posture, hayfeverish.
Face, stepping backwards.

The nights are getting close together,
shallow ends fill and empty and pick a side
but your service words still loop the loops they always did.

It's intermission soon
so we're hurdling the weekend seaside
in a big daft caravan, with a fortune of anecdotes to spend.

How cold is it outside? It's not warm.
Should we bring a coat? Maybe, but then again,
we might just be alright.

Lucy Holt

Breakfast

in the margin of the morning we are on holiday
the coughing men and coffee men are buffered awake
by bad radio hair and the cold bathroom alarm

    tolerated here in chunks of ten and fifteen at a time
    on the wrong side of the crack, and heading further inland
    everything sounds pretend

        it's not ours for the using, not this bit
        you can try to catch the night off-guard, before it's ready to leave
        but every start is a trespass in this other, retreating place

            yesterday's overspill car park is full
            but we still bite back and take pieces out to save for later
            how long can you hold your breath for? I bet it's no longer than this.

Lucy Holt

abstract #2

'Abstract' is a word which is now most frequently used to express only the type of outer form of a work of art; this makes it difficult to use it in relation to the spiritual vitality or inner life which is the real sculpture.
— Barbara Hepworth 'Sculpture'

(i)

pavan (unfinished prototype)

the dressing gown of water drips to my feet
revealing the journeys that you didn't take
as my aluminium gauze body wasn't safe
in the place where the Mobius twist meets

I still long for your yellow plastic car
to fasten onto one of my Scalextrik ribs
dance around me and tightly grip
while someone else squeezes the trigger

(ii)

hollow form with inner form (plaster)

I am the walnut in your dreams
that doesn't open properly
refuses to unclutch the kernel

drowns its brown brain shell
in brilliant white gloss
to camouflage in snowdrops
a cloud of hands

the way I am fashioned
reveals the journey
broken nail wedged in parapet
the two holes an attempt
to make me breathe

(iii)

three forms in Echelon (a maquette)

they communicate arrive by magic
held together by six strings
salvaged from an abandoned banjo
planted under papier maché skin

there is something in its way
an almost curve appears
two wires meet
do not touch

ear shaped archipelagos
how I long to be reborn
as a leafcutter ant
scurry across your almost lobe
creep along the metal ropes
the weight of nature like a flag
against the kingdom of your scaffold

Gary Hughes

cocaine in the saltshaker

after Chaplin's 'Modern Times'

You don't know why your head can't stop
following the spin of the lighthouse bulb.
Everything works within these circles;
the umbral fingernail triggers the curved

flick of gruel into a selfish eyeball.
You remember the dream as a factory fish,
swimming through the cogs of water
until the pressure pushed you out of sync

into the back of the ambulance,
forcing you to renounce every pattern
even those on the linoleum flooring.

Gary Hughes

a Rothko

use me to pretend your brain is somewhere else
washing through cloud crumbling through coastal shelf
or operating in the black between the welcome mat
and the oxygen from the house plant

I'll throw my sieve skin over those I love
snatch it back the scratching proves
that semi-permanence exists
in the building of palimpsest

come scrape your copper against me
will we bronze together
will my white be silver or milk

as the acrylic grinds up frenzied
have you here the dehydrated weather
or crushed up speckled pills

Gary Hughes

On Latch

They went daily,
the latch flying on behind them.
A moment's assurance
for their uncertainty.
They were uninvolved,
but tied in knots.
A pair of shoes — odd —
tumbling over each other.
There goes the latch
and out they come,
a little crooked,
smelling of confusion.
There's nothing
to consider now.
We'll talk about it later.

Aidan Jenner

Mindful

There are body fishers circling your island, dragging up and selling on
the decrepit spirit cages that drowned beneath your whirlpool fractures
entranced by your siren swansong to drift amongst their sea of failings
you're planning which Cerberus head to feed next,
whom you'll entertain with your hourglass experience
and which haggard jigsaw scrap shall hack itself apart
to live awhile amidst your maddened masterpiece
how have you gone so long caressing self-deceit
how can a vegetarian devour so much meat
and why can you not drown me, I'm no Samson
no anchor to harbour your detachment
you are wayward and weathered and impossible to define
tightrope walking along the borderline;
my nightmares envision you falling

Sam Kendall

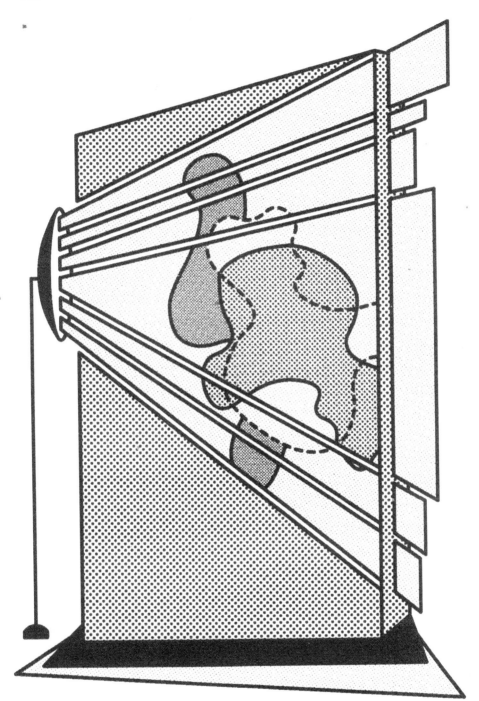

Aer

a white, rectangular room. nothing of its rectangulari ty makes
it whiter than other rooms. nothing of its w hiteness enhances that
rectangularity. it contains no windows, balusters or motifs; these
cannot be contai ned. its air is kept at a constant temperature and
flow -rate. those objects within count days by clicking hee ls, unseen
clocks. when they have only themselves to see they marvel at each
other for uninterupted hours.

Joshua Lingard

Aqua

countries are

fucked fortresses.
new possibilities expressed in spaces once inaccessible.
cities weeping at their reflection.
floes running into culverts.
seeing those who died where you stand.
hammocks sleeping shadow.
avalanches.
young buildings overlooking flatland.
water oozing into channels.
bleeding children — occupying their past, present and future
selves — skating on pillars.
polarised skin repelling in the glassy silence of infant towns.

Joshua Lingard

Ignis (Joan of Arc)

Joan's hair falls, rises. Her body is a casket heaving against earth. The spirit is secular. The feet are sustai ned. The clavicles are flanges. Eyes are fixed plates. The spine is perpendicular to a pyre. Her lips and cal ves are a festival of meat. Her nipples. The lower ba ck-estuary. Her torso. The chin and nostrils are pears. Ears are paper-thin. The inner thighs are an archipe lago, cracked walnuts and a burning chapel. Knee-ha lf-moons. The head and feet are poles. Central Europ e is chest and ribcage. Her waistline assumes the equ tor's width. The palms are the Americas and Asia. Fr

ance is the heart.

Joshua Lingard

Silentium

Take silence by the throat and it speaks.
A crowd packs into a theatre's entrance.
Intertitles bring to lips words that speak in image.
The plasticity of letters holds a resonance alien to the spoken word.
They are consoled with never-before-felt sensations.
Their predecessors had gasped at trains that, they believed,
would tear the screen apart.
Within a dreamscape of acrossness without ups an ocean is
the sum of its peaks, and a moon is dragged from its mineral bed.
Time — the metronymic — is entertainment: it can be slowed
to a stop, sped to frenzy.
Disavowals of nature are composition.

Joshua Lingard

Terrae *(For another)*

Her fingers spread   across
the back of her head. Her knuckles are flat to the bonnet and
elbows at fourty-five degrees to where bonnet meets head.
The trajectory of her thighs in sunlight. The aurora of her
sunglasses reflected in a windscreen. The solar flare of her
cigarettes. Her gravity. The eclipse of her body fusing with
automobile. The black hole of the mouth; tongue against the
dark matter of the palate. The silhouette of her arm reaching
incrementally to the sky. The sky. The word. The word. She
looks to isolate what makes it sky and not a jug or glue,
unpicks stars and planets from its fabric. Still she has not *seen*
the sky. She is weary of rooms — the city's growing pains.
Nothing happens in rooms or cities. She holds a grape
between thumb and finger. It is larger than Venus. The
evidence of our being, she said, will be covered over. There is
romance in that.

Joshua Lingard

Cold Caller

Take comfort in the resonant fact
that we are all of us porous.
Precipitation finds its way inside,
no matter the sediment layered above.
Its chilling course parts each grain
without effort, ever seeping through.
Even the promised shelter of your upturned
collar is no match for the cold caller.

Beneath your navy Harrington the fragile
warmth of your skin is sapped by each drop.
Some ethereal force guides these glistening shells
to their mark, regardless of your evasive manoeuvres.
One by one an army of bristling troops gather themselves,
though their cause is blind.
Slowly and then all at once they quiver
and drown by the deathly embrace of the cold caller.

A doorstep finds its way beneath
the rubber sole of your left foot.
The faded white squeaks weakly against
the damp stone, warning you.
Through a decaying lace curtain
an energy-efficient glow permeates.
It seems to reach out to you,
as if to ward away the clammy approach of the cold caller.

Your naked finger rests
upon the worn brass of the doorbell.
Depressed, it primes itself to alert those inside
to your watery presence.
An involuntary shiver releases the hounds,
and you almost turn tail and run.
Glued to the spot you remain,
in her eyes, a cold caller.

William Lloyd

TANK

After Pierre Jean Jouve

my martian machine
—double-jawed tower—
with your fiery skull
where lives man's calculus

from your sides, middle and back crackle shrapnel,
shells, life-devouring bullets,

you march over earth,
upon the living, dying and dead,
compress the trench beneath your jounce
as you'd close two sides of a wound,

blind beast
rampant in the battle's blast,
beyond even the vanguard;

—inside,
the heroes,
padded up to the nines,
hurling at the walls, smashing their courses;
firing and killing on all sides,
burnt by the torrid heat of engines,
deafened by the din of exploding iron:
living their last day

here is the child of their divine-brain
here the clarity of their bright world

Martin Malone

GHOSTS OF THE VORTEX XIII:
Reconstruction

Audience Notes for Mametz Wood, where — during the course of this large-scale, site-specific production — you are guaranteed a vivid glimpse of our becoming through death. Check availability at the online store and if you're coming, use SatNav only as a guide. From all directions you'll end up on a single track with an uneven surface, so walk, don't run. Supported by public funding through various bodies, this is a sold-out show. Late then, I'll not make it myself but me and the lads will be there in spirit; we'll hold our absent tongues and chip in the odd chit of bone. Strictly speaking, the age guidance is 14+ though, with these things, you could always lie.

Martin Malone

GHOSTS OF THE VORTEX XII:
Emilienne

Can't sing a note, not even the *Marseillaise* — oh, I'll give it a go when occasion demands — but I did have the X-Factor they were looking for. Once the press got hold of it I was an overnight sensation: the 'Heroine of Loos', a new Joan of Arc. Golden *salons*, cocked hats, bemedalled generals and the public square, as the ballyhoo broke over me. At seventeen I was that month's face-of-the-war, mounting the 'Staircase of Heroes' to the *Panthéon*, blazing my brief comet of a season. Sold an exclusive to *Le Petit Parisien* and got locked in some chateau to homespin thoughts for the nation. My reason for telling you? I'm not even writing this.

Martin Malone

Benu Bird

Silence.
Water.
Being and nothingness.

Then Benu.
Benu birthed itself;
wings split the firmament.

Listening, it heard the still-dark.
It cried to hear no other cry.
Shattered and shard-rent.

Bright Benu broke the silence:
keen and crystal, Benu spoke 'Be',
and the world unfolded.

At the cry the hill and forest,
by the cry the river and desert,
of the cry the wide spaces.

Where Benu was was light.
Beaming dawnlight, firstlight.
Casting dark as skimming pebbles.

Each day the ascent;
clawing the sky to feel it trickle fingertorn,
bubbling treacle-soft.

Dim the hour
and falling waterward.
Perish now, tomorrow springs exulting.

Far off and shadow-close,
the echoes evanesce
and nascent silence blooms.

Alex Marsh

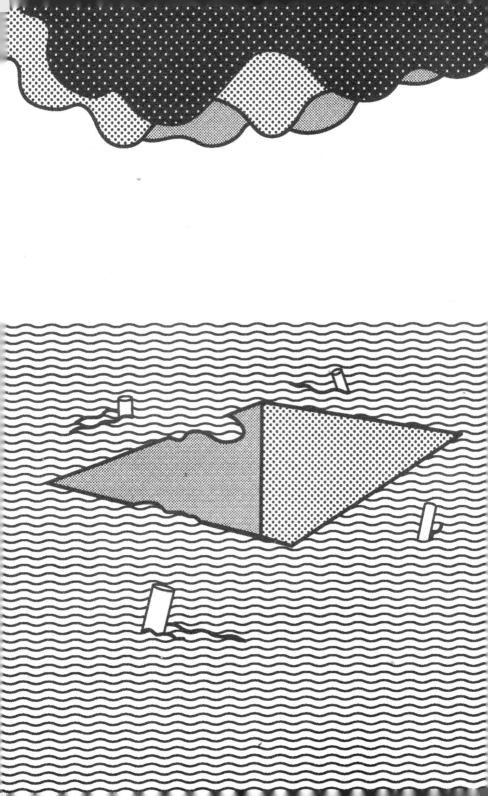

Blodeuedd

I came to you blossom-born;
you plucked me careless from the earth
as I slept, lulled by the
slow-sung,
deep-down,
root-music
that is too soft for your rude ears.
I felt safe until you arrived.

You saw beauty in the broom and
oak-flower,
meadowsweet small and innocent.
Sweet little flower-face,
mixed up in a great cook-pot

Human women surrounded you,
all sweating and dirt-rubbed,
smelling faintly of lamb fat and work.

My mud was only rubbed
from my flesh when I woke.

Your hunched parents declared
'He is too perfect, my boy
for their calloused claws.
Their teeth are too crooked,
their skin too porous,
their bellies too round from roast meat,
and their thighs meet in the middle.
None of them shall have him.'

So they made me;
an artificial thing, newborn
and oh-so-perfect as you,
my Lleu.

I would bear only the scent of lilies,
turning the air funereal and death-heavy.
My belly would never swell,
subsisting on pure light and longing.

I am preserved, pressed
like lilacs,
with powders painted,
gilded
made-up.
A fiction for you.

But one day I will leave you,
painful as the spear in your side.

Alex Marsh

Changes

Wind ruffles
the face of Ukushima.
Waves bloom, lost.

You lay beneath the surface, restless,
dreaming that you would no longer be
a dragon, a slick-scaled ghost beneath the waters.
Cry out to the night; a roar —
crop-withering, earth-shaking.

A caterpillar,
knowing nothing of its future,
weaves a chrysalis.

Wake. Stretch the ache of sleep
from your muscles, corded
beneath your skin like iron.
Flex your killer's claws, remember —
your body has betrayed you.

Upon a cherry branch
the butterfly pauses,
remembering its earthbound life.

Try to forget the brute creature
of your birth. The transition is painful,
chemical, but dreaming is worse.
Be a bird instead; fletched with gold,
shot through the air with an arrow's speed.

Blood is the deepest of dyes;
washed from the surface,
it remains.

The scalpel breaks your flesh, surgical and cold.
Emerge, leaving the husk of your former self
coiled in the deep — a cocoon abandoned,
a grave marker. Rise heavenward;
the sky is empty, beckoning.

Birth betrays us.
Limitless potentials narrow,
Become fixed.

Feel the wind churning at your stroke,
open your beak for an exultant song.
Listen, and despair.
Hear that your voice is still
the bass growl of the beast.

Touch the skin.
Feel it yield to the fingers,
mutable.

Alex Marsh

Swiftness

Take for example the swift;
it has two small eyes,
two wings, two feet,
one beak, bifurcated tail,
careful array of feathers.

Now, in the mind's eye,
remove the feathers.
Not so that it is without feathers,
but such that it was never-feathers.
Now the tail, de-tailed,
the beak — never-beak.
Next the wings, unwinged,
the feet, the little eyes.

They are not necessary;
something else swifts the swift.
Unbodied, it is *swiftness* —
a parabola described upon the sky,
the idea of the swift takes wing.

Alex Marsh

Icarus and Eve in the Playground

In the beginning their see-saw is balanced
with naked toes still weighted down,
brushing the sprung recycled ground. Then Icarus sinks into

a seat-drop
knees-bend
shove

and takes his sister by surprise. In the air
she grabs the cool-curved bar in front of her,
a red-lady, scarlet-woman, pinkish colour, then

sudden drop
her knees jar as
soles hit the rubber

      and Icarus is sailing against the sun-riddled sky.

Jealous, Eve kicks off again,
makes sure to pop his arrogant grin.
He plummets to Earth and now she's perched
all queen-of-the-castle and here-to-stay
      until

      it's not long before they realise
      that they don't know how to stop

      each child wails
      a helpless terror
      as they brutalise each other
          (muscle spasm)
              flight
        then
                 plunge
      and the sharp slap of feet
               taking off again

Catriona McLean

Coiled under Mont Blanc, the Mer de Glace

'I ought to be thy Adam; but I am rather the fallen angel, whom thou drivest from joy for no misdeed.'
— The Creature

The mountain shrugs; detritus falls
into the arduous march of a glacier.
Ice, aspiring to a river's vitality,
lurches and annihilates everything.

Victor suspects the sublime horror
in his son's face — the waiting snake —
as muscles contort to an attempted benevolence.
Under such pressures

the dirt-smeared skin splits;
stress fractures reveal a glistening and wet flesh;
clear, abrasive liquid sluices through the wounds
and carves shining tracks in the brown moraine.

Under such pressures, the apple skin tears:
the sublime reduced to hunger, thirst, fear.

Catriona McLean

Eve

You are almost a stranger,
Holy Mother,
and I am still licking the tart taste of apple
from my fingers as we traipse

the streets of Rome.
You readdress my self-indulgent fall
while perched on a museum bench;
we bury each milestone

inside the convoluted map. Cobbled alleys
narrow our impulses to mere hunger,
thirst. My legs are stronger but together
we choose

to emerge from this transported city into sunlight
with our shadows blurred together in the spaces between monuments.

Catriona McLean

Eyrie

At the low curve of the dive
the earth will rush up
and explode into a brooding mass —
to the heft and march of brute peaks.

At the eagle's whim and smug rise
the mountain's thrust is diminished to
a white repose, a lazy slumber,
an empty contour

conquered with a wave. From this height
the land between each horizon nestles
in the width of his span: the bird
in the dead nest, toying with his miniatures.

The sheer depth irons creases from seas;
seclusion turns all distance to abandonment.

Catriona McLean

Curating

your dank hair trails
her skin. Catches
lashes. Refracted
lamplight scattering
their faces

in mosaic
false warmth then
swathes of ethereal
blue shadowing
the slants of your starved out
features

her legs bowed like
two curving
two dun whittled bones
You refiguring
the smooth translucence
of a limb
the netted black purple vein
in their crescents, shadowing
her echoing stare

She hates my wan little
upward look and
the sweet sweat
laced neck I'm sick for
and after, the way
I chewed you over
the way your
numberless ghosts sat
behind my eyes
as I spoke.
The fractured angles
of your gaze pinning me
to dead minutes

Amber McNamara

The Book

The Book you devoured
Is left scattered in tatters
All you have now
Are chewed up fragments
Caught between your teeth
And a few shreds of
Reality
Pinned down
Forked through the heart

Bridie Moore

Midsummer

I'm waiting for the year to turn
Holding my breath as the globe
On its axis tilts
Towards what? No
Away from the sun

The pregnant year
As the earth moves away
Gestates.
Fruit, will come
At a later date

Now the birds sing
And all is poised on promise
Where are we going?
Back around to the beginning again.

Bridie Moore

Full Stop

Your helmet like a black round mark
Was still in place, marking the end
Marking the place where you
Came to your abrupt conclusion
A sentence uncompleted
Cut short in

And we pass by you
Hurtling forward on to the road
Hardly time to grab hold of scraps of you
To take with us over the swell
Where you will be left behind
Cut off in

The force and fullness of you
Could not be held in a single statement
You would get to the end before you
Got to the end, the gathering energy
Rolling you into a premature stop.

Bridie Moore

Alport Castles

The wind let the landscape move
how it always wanted to,

leaned us together
like ferns, or upper branches

and we walked the slope
believing we were part of the scenery

talking about music and summits,
places we'd never go again.

Then the rocks finished my sentence —
tall and architectural:

their moat of grass
their keep of clouds,

more intricate than any human fort.
We sat up high and praised

like two off-duty gods
as if a view was something

made. And the clouds
over Derwent mended

and we were briefly glorious,
though neither of us had
built, would build a single thing.

Helen Mort

Midday Moon

The sky's a scratchcard
and this shadow is your prize.
As if you thought too hard
and rubbed the clouds away.
You're walking slower than you should
up Woodhouse Lane. You've won
but nothing seems to do you good.
The day holds you like rain
and every question you could ask
won't come, or comes like this wrong moon.
Your lucky stars all whistled past
and left this new thing hanging over you.

Helen Mort

Six

I lay there a candidate cat, snoozing, allowing
your jumbled words to flow over me. A fever
from the fireplace takes my attention from

your hands and words spilling over cirrus clouds.
In our garden Goaty is dreaming of warm woods
and you growing roots in the dry French earth.

Your features rearranged into a stone wall, labouring.
I fly, your stream lined fingers are my bow. Wasps
settle on my round shoulders and I sting them with

my ignorance. You're still talking about canals and barges,
I am inside my ivy pool drowning spiders. The cat slinks in
across trains of goodbyes and your temples open its doors.

I try to sweep myself under the dark wood bed but as
a splinter I'm stuck under your thumb. You are trying to tell me
all I know is already done.

Colombine Neal

Albatross

This iris is clouded with myths;
the creatures which in fear massed together.
In vain we built a home.

Stretched then fractured, I was lifted up.
One wing my conscience, strung up in the chime
of the bells, the cobbles, the Grand Tower.

Another wing my yearning, buried deep
in bracken lands, where a voice still rests
within the Moors' wishing wells.

Diving past spirits, weightless
I watched, for an instant, an angelfish pass
We fell in love, he left, in a storm

carrying throngs of belief, on rapids, like birds
migrating from mind to body
in their thousands.

I wished to love as an albatross, my feet
upon the channel, cautiously waiting
for the surface to break.

My memories drowned in the pass of
deep water, infantile at least.
Before the elements got restless I once

pursued tigers, in a bamboo forest
swam with wasps, as my bower
breathed the sun, through the earth.

He wrote music, she the world;
I was born to a home.
Intact

Colombine Neal

Eyes, this is where she wanted to begin

Eyes, this is where she wanted to begin
openings into more than the present

Skin, not even his, only her own
and breath, heavy breathing

Fingers, digging holes, not holding
a pig for slaughter, still crackling

A jaw slack-lined across the ground
and she once believed her skin

was impenetrable, cold particles
reflecting everything but herself.

If it could all be scraped off
she'd grow feathers and then eyes.

I can't remember his eyes
all I could see was skin

A frail layer
barely an attempt.

Colombine Neal

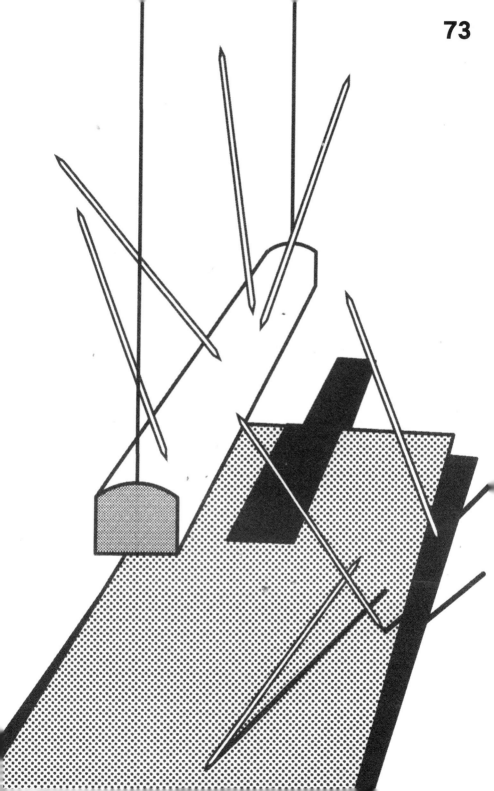

Sitting in the Most Ordinary Room

From 'Four Frames of Reality'

I lift up my cup.
It has a stain,
brown or yellow the moment tells me.
I drink some coffee.
The black liquid feels light on my tongue
and I swallow.
I put the cup back on the table,
let it mark the wooden surface.
I smile through my beard.
The window besides me is broken in three places
and it's dirty.
It doesn't open,
hasn't in nine years.
I feel old when I push the keys on my typewriter
but I continue.
I mistype and throw the white mess against the window.
It sways through the air for a little while
until it bothers me again.
I hit it once more, 'get away from me words of
nothingness!'
I yell in my brain.
The paper lands on the bed, next to her.
She pushes it off the mattress with her breath
and it falls down on the carpet.
My carpet smells.
It makes me as sick as its green color.
I drink some more coffee.
And some more.

After a while,
the light of the two working bulbs
are joined by the sun.
They mumble in the background
as I continue to write.
I mistype again and beat another paper to death.
I send it through the air with great force,
watch it crash against the light blue cloth of her jeans.
My nipples start to freeze
and I realize that I am not wearing a shirt.
I drink some more coffee.
One of the books on my shelf falls down,
almost wakes her.
The door gets jealous and tries on its own.
I sneeze and the white walls shake.
A pain grabs my left rib
and I lean down on my cold radiator.
The blank white page is staring at me,
screaming for color.

Mattias Ostblom

Feeding the Day

His fingers moved slowly from side to side,
shot down like roots in the sea of thick brown hair.
They swept across in full motion,
caressing each and every inch of the boy's skull.

Just below them on the grassy turf
birds picked and pecked through the dirt,
searching for the breakfast meal
of a six-legged creature.
Over at the water fountain
two small rainbows dove around in circles,
craving attention
for the briefest of moments.

He pulled out a handful of black sunflower seeds
from his right jeans pocket.
He opened the palm of his hand, delicately
like a wrapped Christmas present
and gestured the boy to dig in.
The boy scooped up the seeds,
placed them from one hand into the other
and let them rain down on the colorful birds.

There they sat, the father and the son,
watching the birds, listening to the water fountain
and laughing in each other's company.

Mattias Ostblom

What We Learn
When We Learn the Hard Way

Anna holds hot coals in her hands like snow
the first day it falls. In November sun
she is all teeth and goosepimples and
apple pie and eyes the shade of leaves,
and you fit her name around your mouth
like the instruments you never learnt to play.
Anna is the ghost of left behind gloves
and school science experiments and
sometimes she comes home drunk, smiling,
smelling like the first book you ever read.
You swear she could spread her arms so wide
the world would beat in her chest.
She looks for you in the garden and you tell her
about the birds you saw fight amongst the trees.
How the feathers fell blood-matted and wild and
you buried the vanquished in an unmarked grave,
so number 8's cat couldn't reap the spoils of war.
And Anna laughs and smiles and understands
because she's swallowed more loss than
a casket can carry.

Ellie Pearce

'Equalizer'

Arms clasped at the dip of his spine
smooth against the silk sheen of his waistcoat —
bowler hat tipped.
He watches two sons ride one enamelled steed
of the galloper carousel.

The horse's feet never touch the ground,
steamed-up, they go round like a zoetrope —
under the mushroom spokes of the awning.
The father's shadow laid out in front
like a drunk man in the Hall of Mirrors.

One of these boys, forty odd years on,
will flutter a betting slip that breaks him,
watching his jockey-less nag cross the line
that keeps running until lathered.

Karl Riordan

Paternoster

We hop on at ground level and ascend
hand in hand
all the way to the eighteenth
to play in the clouds
and look out to Neepsend.
Like someone threading the rosary
going round on the Hail Mary's.
At the fourteenth to sixteenth
I went past, hair all Vaselined,
to all mussed up.
We turn at the top
as if moving on a blueprint.
On the way down like a morning
in a pit shaft
where language changes from home.
You step out at the mezzanine
leaving me to keep sinking
past ground to basement
with a split decision, where to get off.

Karl Riordan

Recipe

Back from fishing he's upstairs tipping
live eels into a full bath,
writhing into figures of eight.
Listen to him cursing with the thud
of the fisherman's priest dashing down.

Mags is frying onions for his Dublin Coddle—
handkerchief optional.
Sear the pork until browned,
mix with stock,
carrots and layered potatoes.
Bring to a simmer,
sprinkle with ground glass.
Leave to stew until meat is tender
or crabbit husband clatters home from pub.
Stir occasionally, season to taste.

She flinches at his reflection
over her shoulder, combing up his hair.
Unlit cigarette attached to his lips,
zipped up jacket sounds the only farewell.
Down the path he turns up his collar,
pushes the gate outwards into the street
like swinging into a Western saloon.

Sit the supper tray onto his lap,
place remote into open palm,
quietly pull the ball-catch on the door.

Karl Riordan

Hail Mary

And while his father was in the shop
buying cigs, chatting up the cashier,
he reached for the family claw hammer
and smashed the dials of the white van,
going at the mileage they'd done,
the speed at which they'd travelled to get here.
It occurred to him
that things would not be the same from this point.
There'd been other signs:
rashers pegged out on the washing line,
the mystery of the garrotted dog.
The rosary hanging from the mirror
is unhooked, and each bead is threaded
through finger and thumb.
He sees his dad exit the shop, smile,
tap a cigarette on the ingot pack
click and spin the Zippo on his thigh, exhale.

Karl Riordan

More Seed than Flesh

We crushed blackberries inside empty butter tubs
becoming inky palm stained scholars,
smiling through smeared war paint
as we unpicked seeds from between our teeth
and blackened fingernails.
We were unaware of the liquid lacing us together
binding berries with spit.
An invisible thread looped through my front teeth
then beneath his tongue.

Later, after the grass
had laughed from yellow to green
and back again,
we crouched in that same spot.
This time we did not tumble backwards.
We fell forward.
Our lips brushed and tongues touched
tasting lukewarm evening sun
and blackberries.
Bent down in a curious curtsy
making imprints
as if we were sculpting clay.
My knees aren't muddy now
they aren't grazed and bloody now.
I did not feel dirty.

Later, after he had replaced me
or I him.
The next kiss
worked its way through me
like a palm hammering hard from the wrist.
My spine locked with the pine's spine
zipping us together.
Bark bruised me with its lattice pattern
barbed wired branding
my skin of satin.
Overgrown limbs
grappled with my undergrown hips.

Trapped in the brambles
where there are no blackberries.
Except for one.
You try picking her
she is unripe
and leaves a bitter taste
on your sandpaper tongue.
My knees weren't muddy
not grazed or bloody.

Katie Smart

Night Guard

Twisting your swan neck into a hook
bent from your spine
forced down eye line.
Feeling branches brush the nape of your neck.
Appreciating the affection.
You cannot snap your head back
to see who caresses you.
You were made with the purpose
to help others observe
and not to be the observer.
With one unblinking eye
watching the same
static ground.

At your feet
a graveyard of leaves
their veins once pumped full of life from rain
wither into empty stencils.
Scuffling feet scatter
making the skeletons dance
they disturb the bones and laugh.
You want to look away.
You stare.
Stare as a shy child stares at shoelaces in strange company.
You almost wish you could whisper,
cry out
you have no mouth
just one unblinking eye.
You stand to attention.

A palm strangles you,
sweat dribbles like condensation.
To them you smell like rust and blood.
Shuffling feet
swaddling arms
swaying bodies, embracing.
You wonder what it is to be embraced.
You remain chaste.
In night you shine
have you ever saved a life?
You don't know.

You wish to snap back your head
shatter that carefully constructed curved neck.
Veins running through you
have always been dead.
Wires.
Live wires are not alive.
You stare with your solitary eye.

Katie Smart

Scales

Basking in the reddish glow of fishing boats
you squeeze your heels together,
wishing your white shoes red
willing the warmth of home.
          And you receive it.
Splashing in waves of your brother's blood.
They bathe you in rubies.
Your gills try stealing oxygen
from porphyrous puddles.
Your skin congealing, forming scabs
from wounds which aren't yours.
Lapping at your non-clavicle
the tepid kiss of used life.

Basking in the reddish glow of fishing boats
you feel like Roxanne.

          Untangle my fishnet stockings
          peel back my scales
          and gaze upon my Magdalen flesh.
          Mary, Mary quite contrary

to belief
we enjoy the feast.

Katie Smart

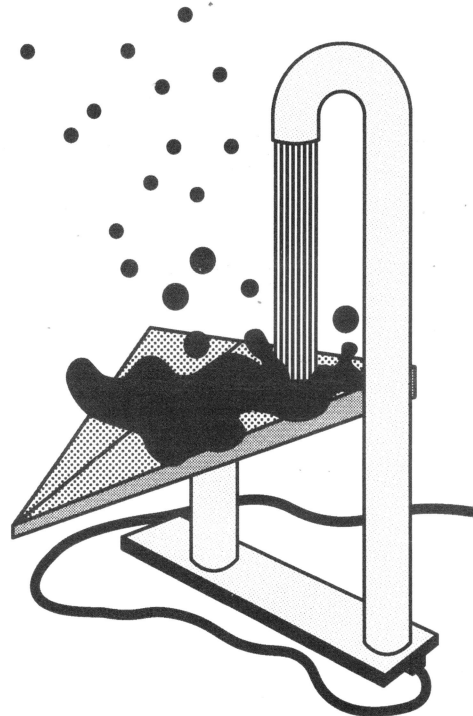

Lunar soliloquy

[Howling]   I'm a werewolf
that keeps throwing on human clothes
in hopes of morphing back.
[Snarling]   But none of these socks fit.
And it's hard to undo buttons with claws,
[Whimpering]   nobody will lend me their clippers.
I think I might just curl up in a meadow
of forget-me-nots
blooming ravenously for remembering.
[Yawning]   And maybe I'll howl at the moon
another night,
when I don't feel so lethargic.

Katie Smart

Cover Me in Feathers

Give me pigeon feet
complete with missing toes.
I want a pigeon beak
to hide my human nose.
Cover me in feathers
my own protective layer.

Give me pigeon wings
they can watch me go.
I want pigeon eyes
to see what they know.
Cover me in feathers
my own protective layer.

Give me pigeon bones
with all the different joints.
I want a pigeon heart
in a rib cage that conjoins.
Cover me in feathers
my own protective layer.

Give me a pigeon head
complete with birdy brain.
Then I could forget
free from human pain.
Cover me in feathers
my own protective layer.

Wings sprout from my shoulder bones
never hold you, hear you moan.
At least, at last I'm free
from you, your indifference.
You always hated pigeons.

Covered in feathers
my protective layer.

Katie Smart

Eclipse

'Look at the sunset,' they said. 'Isn't it beautiful?'
But when I turned, it had already sunk.

'Look at the sunset,' they said. 'Do you see it?'
I squinted, trying to peel its flame from the sky.
Then a cloud blew it out.

So they tied a knot around the sun and anchored the rope to the ground.
One long, orange day followed.

The rope frayed, the sun ballooned away and darkness swallowed the sky.

Cowering in silvery shadows, I turned.
The moon lifted my chin.

Lucy Smith

Venetian Vultures

Stern steps pounded the paved ground
as my father turned away.
Bridged canals creeping past our crumbling façade
of a happy family, he clenched his fists
and marched onward.

Halted by no man, marriage or wife,
he tore through pastel streets
like a vulture to slaughter,
complete with thinning hair,
a baggy suit, and hunched shoulders.

My mother, the raven, followed behind.
Carrying baggage and searching
for greying skies, finding only windows
barred by panes, pain, and corrugated iron.

And I slouched behind.
A dove, or pigeon, trying to peacock
my way into their sight, to steal a glimpse
or a moment in any way I could.

Wings clipped by pocketed hands,
I skimmed alongside the raven
as the vulture tore ahead.

Nathan Spencer

Dusk on the Logging Road Below Tumbledown and Little Jackson

Clouds, the dry cups,
the mountain lamps.

The pause that follows
the slipping away, slipped away sun,

our petals
of blood carried down

dark galleries
to the cupboards of summer.

A trickling perdition
at the road edge, our exhaustion

as crickets
build their pillars.

We move among the second causes.

II

Earlier and still ourselves we tramped
the chimneys of Maine,

along green eaves,
sky–sides and shingles.

We heaved ourselves
over the outcrops like trunks

of soul, we beat ourselves
like rags against the boards,

we bit into peaches
and the rivers

ran along our necks, by the blue rivers
of our necks,

the many rivers.

David J Troupes

The Man Behind the Gas Station Counter

What a strange six months it had been! And now it was Christmas morning, back at the family home, up early and out of the house, just myself alone in the years-later vacancy, the old streets. Air like a spent avalanche, a slackwater of time. Night wasn't ended—merely bleached.

You begin to doubt yourself, sitting at a computer all day, looking at numbers which tell you a line is being gouged from the Gulf of Mexico right up to Canada, through forests where you are not, under mountains where you are not. To leave at lunch and spend thirty minutes walking the bank becomes a kind of confrontation. Here is the river, moving, and you beside it likewise—and you must choose between your moving self here and your still self sat lustily inside.

I drove along Main Street, past filthy squirts of three-week snow, to the gas station by the highway exit. The plan was to buy a few more gifts for my mother's stocking, something I had put off for no reason. The man behind the counter acted uninvolved as I paid for the Life Savers, pistachios and scented trees which I hoped would not look too obviously like a gas station purchase when she opened them later that morning. I pocketed my change. The coffee here was fresh, the sunglasses were inexpensive. The man behind the counter did not look like the Christmas type, a type which I—despite this morning's poor performance—considered myself to be.

Everything outside was tooth color. I sat in the car a minute, wondering how best to frame this as the loving gesture it was.

A few cars made for the highway.

There is another story I could tell you, about another Christmas morning up early and alone, when I met a coyote in the woods and couldn't say whether I was boxed by windows or mirrors. But that is a story I understand.

David J Troupes

Semantic

Gaping cavern mouth, words forming in wombs
but no labour could push out meanings
as convoluted or inexpressible as these
contractions that wracked minds
and ripping muscle aches

in that moment imagination was enemy
preconception an anticipatory glare
or sweat beads upon the forehead
or gripping fingers on bedrails
digging nails into palms of expectancy

pregnant minds brooded foreboding
scanning grey blurred images moving
fragile shreds that tear like paper
torn roughly from the refill pad
white and waiting black engraving

then miscarried in congealed red
depths in secret insides become violent
inauspicious spitting and bile vomiting
scared eyes rolling and sighs and mourning
sickness in whispers panting infant loss

but exteriors were calm pools in the evening
bridges throw inviting handshakes over the lake
and harness shores together in assuaging truce
and all she said was 'Hello', walking calmly away

Anastasia Van Spyk

Crocodiles

on the television the man said that there are many crocodiles
in the sewers beneath New York
City after saying that he brought the crocodiles out crocodiles
or at least the ghosts of them I could trace
the green and brown of crocodiles
in the long orange current I had to wonder
where it was that the crocodiles were going to at least
where they thought it was they were going
to or otherwise if they had made their home there
among the dirt and had resolved to have their
city there   once I wrote a story about two people they
lived in a sewer underneath a city
there had been a kind of nuclear disaster
that I never really thought through they had no
food or water but still somehow they
survived I think what I was thinking about were
crocodiles and the reason I am so
interested in them today is because of what they
show namely that we can live in a lot of
places even the most unbearable of them I also
think I have thought too critically about
many things   I cannot think through
the world the way a mole or a worm breaks
their way through the ground or a crocodile swims
through a jetsam of death   when I think
my thinking does not leave the world a world intact
it leaves the world a hand with only the skin of its
fingers a boneless hand or a stanza
with no people in it and what good is a stanza
that no one lives in especially when there are
crocodiles living in the swamp beneath New
York City   of course the flow of the poem is the flow
of the current and the rocks made of dirt
that are in it and together we have
swam through the current and now here we are covered
in the world we have swam through   the most
magical type of bike ride is when a bike
ride happens without a bike ever
being ridden

Joe Vaughan

Ghost song

the boy was a ghost the boy was
also a boy his skin was a ghost's skin the length of a
boy's skin it was not transparent and it was not
white there was no flesh beneath
it he had died and had not finished
dying like a download just half
done so that what he ended up with
was a song that was not the
full song   the boy rattled often like a rabbit or a
hamster that had escaped its
cage he opened drawers nervously and
cupboards knocked over china and crockery he
haunted his loved ones the most who he
had struggled endlessly to forget   they called in a ghost
finder who found no traces of
him of course they did not they were a dog
who followed grief for
bones   the boy lived so long that he
watched everyone he had loved
die it was difficult to fall in love
again as a ghost he could
not touch anything or hold anything
or have anything but his own
song the unfinished song
the not complete
song it was a very animal
lyric it carried on
forever

Joe Vaughan

Timber

A web of
whispering limbs
armoured like the sun.

Sun-dappled gilded scales
dance with every murmur,
overshadowing their forebears.

Mighty forms stretch,
striving for a glimpse of a
blinding, ethereal eye.

With the kiss of cold,
their glory is stripped
and they are left.

The chill deepens.

Rusted armour cascades
to crunch beneath
the feet of weaker beings.

Or, it is abandoned,
concealed anew by
a colourless shroud.

Tired of life,
they wait in silence
for the touch of metal.

At the last they feel
curious warm tongues
flaying their flesh.

Sam Wadkin

Poetry?

Grey days what do you do?
Write poetry she said.
Really, like with rhymes and stuff?
No just poetry.
Where does it come from?
Where what?
Where...
I don't know, like the other side of a reflection or something.
How can you see the other side of a reflection?
You can't it's just a figure of speech.
Like a cuckoo's nest?
A cuckoo's... Yeah I guess so. Like a cuckoo's nest.
So poetry is like a willing suspension of the norm?
The norm...? Poetry doesn't recognise a norm!

She wrote these three lines:

Ask not where the other side of a reflection lies,
Or what can reasonably be quantified,
Only where the lines blur in the mind.

I still don't know what she meant.
I doubt if she did either.

William Watts

Pop clichés I can do without

I've never cared for people who say they can't live without you
or for anyone who has presumed to climb a mountain,
or swim an ocean to be with me.

I'm bored of stars being compared to gems and
bored of trying to see those gems in your eyes.
If the sun shines only for you, I'd gladly be nocturnal.

If I am everything you will ever want and
everything you will ever need,
could this be anything but horribly overbearing?

If you really were an angel,
cloaked in dreams and borne by promise,
I'd want only the visceral part of you.

Don't say you will always be there for me;
because always is a long time and
I don't admire the undiscerning.

I'm tired of metaphors of stones worn by the sea.
Maybe the stones aspire to sand,
the way all things tend towards lessening.

William Watts

Settled

She searches for meaning
in the steam of their simmering meal
as he comes in,
quietly smelling of winter's exhaustion.

He busies himself with blown bulbs
and contemplates the crack that
slowly spreads its way up the staircase,
pretending he knows just what to do.

Over dinner she puts into words
the hollowness that's spreading through her
and how she hardly ever feels warm anymore.
He looks at her softly and picks plaster off the wall.

Later they sit side-by-side on a sagging sofa,
feeling the draught that licks its way through their two-bed-terrace.
They lace their fingers together
and watch their breath rise before them.

In bed they knit their limbs together,
ignoring the city's sirens that still make them jump,
he whispers about tomorrow
and how he has all the time in the world but never enough.

Speech slurs to sleep
and suddenly the dark is full of silence.
They dream of realities no more distorted than their own,
whilst dawn waits for them to wake.

Matilda Webb

Nelly

The gingham of your ears
has faded under the weight of
whispered secrets from
sleepless nights.
Where a restless child
tugged gently at your heart
and listened for the soft lullaby that
promised peace.

Your coat has worn thin over time,
through homesick tears,
and the secret squeezes
of a lonely adolescent
when the world seemed too big to bear.

You sit now,
on a dusty shelf,
amongst the shells of ambitious spiders,
with those button eyes,
which know everything (but never see):
a distant spectator.

But in the quiet, empty hours
the dying notes of
'You Are My Sunshine'
can still be heard fading slowly
into silence.

Matilda Webb

Invitation

The invitation is written in viscous ink,
not dark, exactly,
but carrying shadows.

The paper has passed through many hands,
or so people insist.
Historians of the future may
probe its crevasses,
(or its crevices, should someone tell them the difference),
seeking some emblem,
like dusting for fingerprints
on the absence of rock,
or scouring melted snow for a bootmark.

Gaps filled in with lack
obscenely erupt in cold dark nights of soul.
Or we spectate from mountainsides
on frozen mornings to see how the landscape
cracks
and shifts its load from shoulder to shoulder,
a wounded hermit with fraying straps.

The surface has grown deep here,
creaking beneath its inscriptions.
Some corners curl inward and others away.
A beckoning thing.

The anachronistic urgent plea —
'Répondez s'il vous plaît' —
vainly whispered by a silent film star
to inevitable disappointment,
drowning in a key changed by
calloused fingers.
Now just a formless breath,
dissipating in the deaf air.
Artful directors tend not to linger
on sounds that were never there,
or on monochrome lips
made stupid and sad
by infantile muteness.

And so the invitation begins to look less handsome,
like a single leaf on an overhung autumn street,
trod deep into the pavement
by thousands of careless footsteps.
Ink forgets its dry old confidence
and begins to run

Mark Wood

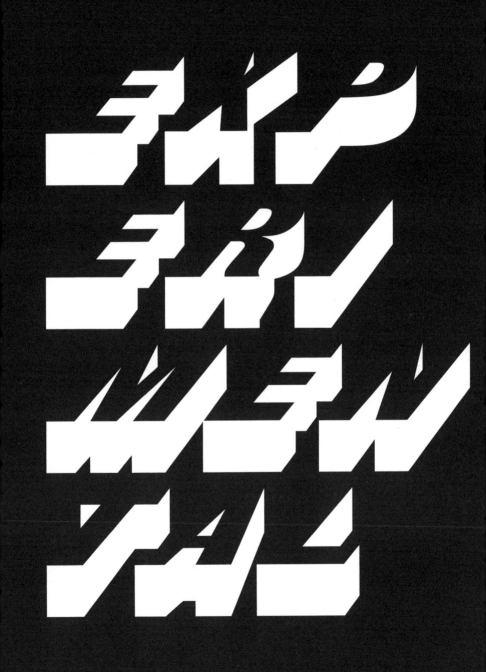

Editors

Sam Ladkin
Mitchel Pass

Untide

untied etude
redundant
untide
detune
persistence

unedit

tenuous confluence

elude united

fugitive desiccation

untide

unedit detune

horizon

etude

component

untied untide

'Untide' was first produced for the online edition of Route 57,
where it can be seen in a larger format coloured version.

Timothy Plant

Editors

Matthew Cheeseman
Camille Brouard
Kiran Dosanjh
William Watts

Revisit Guernsey

Petit Bot

Petit Bot, a beautiful little bay on the South coast, is a popular tourist spot enclosed by picturesque cliffs. As with many of the island's coastal spots, this beach has its fortifications: a grandiose loophole tower, built from Guernsey granite by the British during the eighteenth century to guard against France. The St. Clair battery, jutting out of the cliff edge, was built in the Napoleonic era. The Germans modified these battlements during the WWII Occupation. Nazi troops destroyed two windmills at Petit Bot, fearing their use in a British spy operation as the beach was a prime landing point for invaders wishing to reclaim a British territory captured by the Germans.

We sat up on the cliffs that day, and talked for hours about the arbitrary nature of gender. I began to understand just how trapped you felt here, and why you needed to leave.

St. Peter's Church

The Church of St. Pierre du Bois in Cherbourg was placed under the patronage of the Benedictine Monks of St. Mon Michel in 1030 by Robert, Duke of Normandy. During this century, the parish churches of Guernsey were each dedicated to a saint. French was spoken during religious services until 1927. St. Peter's is often commented on for its sloped aisle. One of the church's stained glass window depicts St. Peter as a fisherman wearing a Guernsey jumper.

I wanted to hold your hand as we edged through the dark, whispering and laughing, but I didn't have the courage. It never would have worked.

Les Cotils

An elegant Victorian country house, this hotel and Christian centre lies in the busy capital parish of St. Peter Port, but is itself tranquil and surrounded by twelve acres of land. Until the German invasion Les Cotils was run by nuns as a school and farm, after which they ran a hospital for the elderly and infirm. Despite a brief break during the war, this continued into the 1980s until the nuns decided to leave due to a lack of members. The building is now a hotel and non-denominational meeting place, which houses a day-care centre run by the local Health Board.

I went once a fortnight to see you in that strange little library, sitting awkwardly and crying in a wingback chair, surrounded by books. I felt like I didn't deserve therapy the first time, but I came here for two years.

Port Soif

Port Soif beach is a hotspot for wildlife as it teems with rock pools. This area is important for the conservation of wetland plant species and it is home to the rare bee orchid and sand crocus, which can be found in the dunes. The beach is shaped like a basin, carved into the coastline and sheltered by grassy headland. Water is let in by a narrow gap between Grandes Rocques and Portinfer.

You sat between my outstretched legs and leaned back into me, your hair brushing against my cheek. I wanted to distil the moment, capture the warm breeze and the sea sounds and the comforting smell of you. I wanted to experience the love and warmth in a never-ending loop.

Sunken Gardens

The Sunken Gardens, known officially as St. James's Gardens, was built into the ground in 1972, after the demolition of St. Paul's Methodist Church. Now the site is a small, green sanctuary for those living and working in town (capital parish St. Peter Port). In April 2009, a team of locals regenerated the gardens, renewing the grass and other plants. Around this time, the local police, stationed a short distance away, declared the gardens an alcohol-free zone in the hopes of deterring vandalism and anti-social behaviour.

I spent nearly every teenage Saturday here, the sunken solace housing an assortment of misfits. That is, when we weren't terrorising the bus terminus or being shooed out of shops. The Sunken Gardens were a microcosm of Guernsey's subcultures: emos smoked with chavs, goths conversed with nerds, and there was even a group called the 'Guernsey Pirates', who dressed for the part and operated on an economy of errand-running and casual violence. Nowadays, it's a popular spot for workers on their lunch. There's even grass again.

Vazon Beach

Vazon is one of Guernsey's largest and most popular beaches among tourists and locals alike. A whole section of its coastline is dedicated to surfers as this point of the island offers some of the best surf in the UK. The Richmond end of Vazon, less popular with beachgoers, is open to dogs all year round, whereas most beaches ban dogs during the summer months. During the summer the beach is closed periodically for sand racing and the road is occasionally closed so that cars and motorbikes can test their luck against the clock, riding reckless on the sun-hot tarmac.

We walked along here after you were put to sleep, soft head cradled by our hands as your breathing faltered and your heavy eyes flickered shut, completely at odds with your usual speed and grace, your endearingly grouchy personality, how you would rest your head on my shoulder. I didn't know how to feel, what to say, as I shuffled up the sandy hill. You were a good dog.

Guernsey Airport

On May 5th, 1939, La Villiaze airfield began to take over prime farmland, causing controversy with locals. It did not open for general use until 1946, due in part to Nazi occupation. The original airport had four grass runways before a tarmac runway was added in 1960. Aurigny Airlines, originating in the neighbouring island of Alderney, began inter-island flights in 1968 from Guernsey Airport, using bright yellow 'Islanders', before moving onto 'Trislanders', expanding flights to Southampton and Cherbourg. In 2004 a new terminal was built and the old terminal demolished for additional aircraft stands. An extension to the runway, causing as much controversy over land as the airport's first incarnation, was finished in 2013.

I was so excited to see you I could barely sit still in my seat.

German Military Underground Hospital

The largest construction on the island, the Underground Hospital in St. Andrews was built by the Germans during World War II. The tunnels, rooms, and ventilation shafts were carved out by slave workers, many of whom died before the hospital's completion. There are still metal fittings on the walls of the operation room and simple pallet beds line the wards. The atmosphere down there is cold, dark and dank. Stalagmites have formed on the floors. Many patients of the hospital were reported to be as white as their own sheets after weeks being treated underground.

You listened as I read aloud the side effects from the thin, unfolded piece of white paper, whilst we sat side by side in the car. I set the box down in my lap slowly, handling the innocuous little pills as if they were powdery explosives. I wasn't sure what they would do. I was afraid to tell my family, trust severed by paranoia and a need to protect myself from their lack of understanding. At that time I barely understood it myself, this illness, but you trusted my judgement, sat in the waiting room when I got the prescription. You gave me the strength I lacked in asserting my need for empathy and support. Thank you.

Camille Brouard

For a street to desire

There are many paths, tracks and roads that come before this street.

I've seen, heard and smelt this street; in fragments, built into my mental geography. Firmly programmed into my software. I can scan the scene and compare against my database that allows me to judge, perceive and predict.

When I was little, I loved the smell of viburnum trees. The ones with the little pink flowers that reek sweetly. As an adult, I now have a favourite viburnum which makes me stop on my corner.

My feet are continually updating my walked narrative. In this way, to put it egocentrically, two completely different times and places are linked by me. To avoid such selfishness, I could've said that *In this way, place and time are articulated via the body, the senses.*

As I've grown older, the appropriation has been reversed in my mind. It's less about imposing my experience on space or a place (being *lived* space). It's become more about the place imposing its own will and wants.

Have you ever considered, for example, that a street's boundaries are defined by territory? Territory which presents itself in the rows of houses that line up either side. It's in the cars parked on the pavement, extending the realm of 'property' to the space of the pedestrian. Territory shows itself every Tuesday when the bins haphazardly line up, dutifully waiting to be collected. A symbol of the rhythm of domestic life, where one person's private is transformed into everyone else's public.

Within these territorial boundaries, the pedestrian is reduced to a linear motion, confined to the pavement. Woe betide the rambler who mistakenly finds themselves down a cul-de-sac (or a bag's arse). These, to me, symbolise the ultimate territorial places. If you are not resident or part of a workforce, you have no business being there.

The gaze of the Big Other feels especially powerful.

These territorial places are a testament to spatial justice: *who receives what and why*.

Streets, being a manifestation of spatial justice, remind us that place is not a depoliticised or neutral phenomenon. It is a product of a decidedly unneutral people.

It's a strange thing for a street to desire, but these days I find myself constantly asking 'what does this space *want*?'

As if I had a choice...

Desire Paths
By a plurality of people meandering off the established path (territory) they forge a way that is oftentimes more convenient and original.
By walking along these I like to think I'm walking in the boots of radical drifters, inhabiting their very line of view.

Emily Reed

Mixed Memories

I had keys, but in the years since leaving home I had taken to ringing the bell so my mother could again compose her flustered face. This time though my father answered the door and in his usual glacial tone said, 'She is in the conservatory getting all... emotional.' It was both a hello and an instruction to go and look after her. I brushed down the corridor filled with pictures from my childhood, all positioned carefully by my mother, who had selected photos in which my unruly hair had been moulded, against the forces of nature, into something visually clean and controlled.

I had never known anyone to make an emotionally unstable wreck look so elegant. She was stretched out on the floor, surrounded by a fortress of photo albums, arm gently resting on the coffee table. She sobbed only occasionally, dabbing the streams of tears so as not to ruin her immaculate make-up. The much awaited photograph set she had ordered from my graduation ceremony had finally arrived.

She was holding a picture from my first ballet exam. Only seven years old. A gap-toothed child, still all the wrong shape, smiling at the camera. 'You were such a beautiful child, I was so proud that day. You were such a star even back then, the most beautiful little child, and how I loved getting you ready for all your dance recitals.'

My memory of that day is quite different. My mother, always the image of perfection amongst her peers, was a winning pie maker and flower arranger who had married the perfect man who in turn had given her three wonderful boys. But I remembered her on the verge of tears moments before I entered that exam hall. Tears of pure distress at her less than perfect child.

The women in her social circles looked up to my mother, the wondrous woman who had so graciously adopted a little mixed race girl. She had told all her friends that she had fallen in love at first sight, regardless of my colour and that she had so wanted a little girl after three boys. In my teenage years it

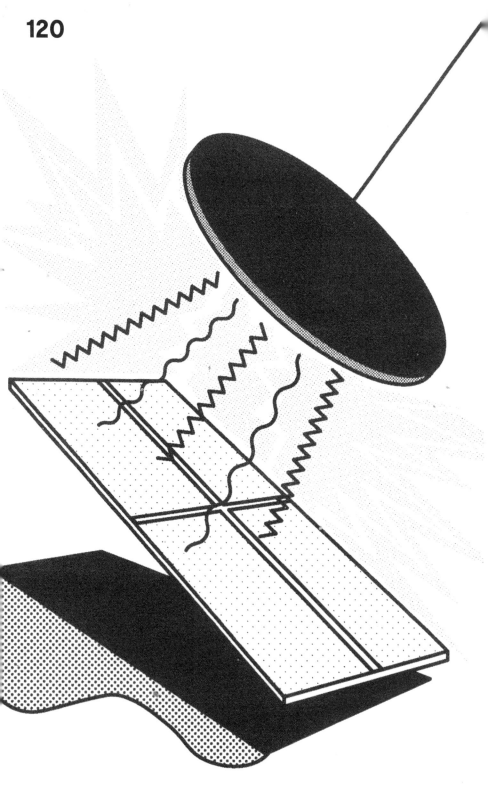

became apparent that I was quite fair for a child with mixed parentage, someone 'like her', as some of my mother's friends would refer to me, though I wasn't entirely sure if they meant adopted or not white (specifics aside, I was different). I always felt that they were silently saying *you did so well with the boys, it must be some of that bad blood she has in her.*

My mother attempted to make me fit in. She had kneaded and moulded me with all her will; the ballet classes, violin, horse riding, all conspiring to form my shell, her image of perfection. She seemed to have forgotten all the precious blonde girls who she looked at wistfully as she dealt with my wild curly locks. The English Rose blusher handed out by my ballet teacher hardly grazed my skin. I seemed to be the only one left with the memory of her shouting on the morning of the exam; pulling the biggest comb she could find through my mane with such gusto she broke several teeth. How could she have forgotten burning me with hot irons she found on a trip to America? All the Sunday evenings spent cross legged as she pulled my hair mercilessly into a failed French plait.

I remember entering the colourless exam room, still surrounded in a cloud of hair lacquer, wincing from the pins shoved into the bun, my thick thighs (from the bad blood) rubbing ever so slightly.

She picked up my graduation picture, and with a final sigh, 'I just wished you hadn't have worn your hair like that. There are ways to control it now.'

Rebecca Solomon

Thrown to the Dogs

Norway looked like it was trapped in a snow globe. Streetlights framed heavy snow in the dense night, dandruff of the sky to my wide young eyes. I was ten years old. We were being driven to a lake in the next village, to be taken on a husky ride.

The Scandinavian Volvo, in its natural habitat, roared up the peak of a hill. At the summit we were greeted by the sight of a dark lake with lamps like Christmas hung around its perimeter.

We pulled in at a dock at the bottom of the hill. From the snug warmth of the car I peered out at our guides. To my child's eyes they were Vikings, dragged out from troll-laden mythology to take tourists on tours of lakes. The huskies were ferocious guard dogs of Valhalla, with all the savagery that comes from burning, pillaging and lapping mead from enemy skulls.

I felt ridiculous in my puffy sky blue snow coat and looked back at my family. The layers they had piled on me made me feel like a Russian doll. I turned back. We were being beckoned out of the car.

Standing on the lakeside, my mind saw every crack and imperfection on the ice. How much would it take to break through; how did they know the ice was thick enough? Caught up in my worries, I failed to notice the rest of my family being led to a sled.

And I was alone.

Left to the mercy of the Vikings and their war dogs.

One of them looked towards me. He burst out laughing, a booming laugh which echoed through my ears. 'Come,' he said, smiling and pulling me towards the husky train.

The convoy was six sledges long, separated in turn by teams of four huskies. At the head of the procession were my family, sat in the sled and wrapped in furs and leathers, looking like candy canes in a stocking. It all became clear. I was just being reunited with my family.

I gave them a wave to show everything was fine.

Then the Viking placed a meaty hand on my shoulder and guided me to an empty sled at the back of the group. He gave me a pat on the back and placed my hands on the bar before me, before departing to his own sled at the front.

Everything was not fine.

I was in charge of four huskies with the bundled, collective energy of a Norwegian blizzard. I could sense their disapproval, their indignation at being saddled with a child. They howled and shifted on the surface of the lake. I was terrified.

The rider in front turned to give me a thumbs up and I suddenly realised: it was a test, a challenge. A rite of passage, my initiation into Viking society. I had to impress. I gripped the reins and dug my feet in. The call came from the front and the dogs powered forward. The trial had begun.

I was yanked on, but kept a steely grip on the bar. Determined in a way only a child who wants to impress can be. We whipped past lamp-lit fir trees and cabins through the heavy night. The barks of the huskies overcame the 'gees' and 'haws' of the drivers as they echoed off the delicate ice, separating the husky teams from the frozen fathoms below.

I was exhilarated now; in charge, bringing up the rear, playing a key role. I was Ben Hur of the frozen wastes, Captain Scott crossing a perilous lake in the name of exploration. I had met the challenge. I felt like one of the tribe. A leader of the tribe.

When we completed the circuit and returned to the dock, I stepped off the sled. Striding through the snow, I gave curt nods to the other drivers who responded with laughter. I didn't mind. I was one of them now. A complete Scandinavian warrior.

As we returned home in the Volvo, my head began to droop under the drone of the engine, and I slept, looting and pillaging.

Jack Stacey

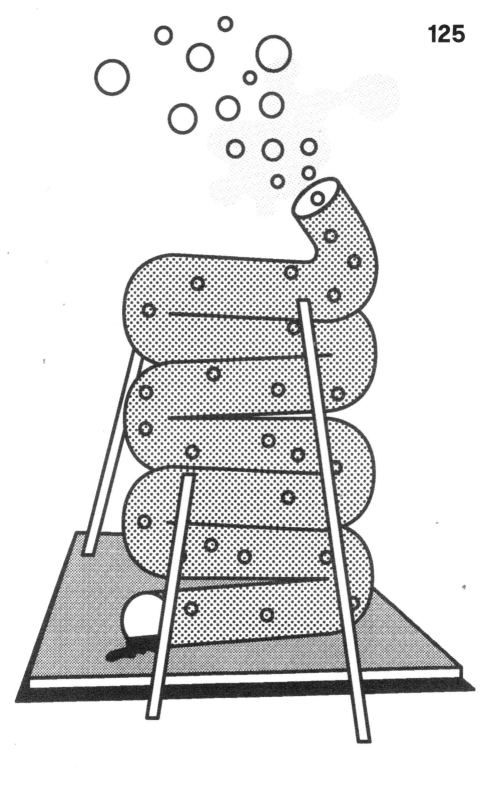

Sixes and Eights

Since I was diagnosed in 2005 I have received a great deal of sympathy, understanding and tolerance from my friends and family, yet I have also been exposed to verbal abuse, antipathy, intolerance, hate, physical violence, disgust and ridicule. The experience of a mental health disorder is a highly personal and varied thing and no two people ever experience the same condition in quite the same way. All I can do is lay down here in words, as best I can, the broken and refracted impressions of my time outside of the normal spectrum of perceived reality, as experienced through the spectacle of my illness.

We all know that feeling you get when you've forgotten something important you were just about to say. It's like that but constant, a blank in which you are continually trying a dig up that key idea that made your entire train of thought make sense. But once the train is derailed it never quite fits back on the track. You will find that your mind is whirring so fast that you can't hold on to your own thoughts, it's like clutching at grains in a sandstorm while it is choking you.

That frog in your throat that you felt when you tried to talk to your upper school crush, it's similar to that except every time you think you have swallowed it, another frog leaps right back up in its place until you feel like you are shitting amphibians, and well you could be, because you no longer have a handle upon what is quantifiably true.

It's a space you get lost in where simultaneously nothing seems possible and yet you can't quite believe anything to be impossible. You are unsure whether or not you did actually once go into space, or unearthed the fundamental truth of existence that could put an end to all philosophical discussion once and for all, and yet the task of getting out of bed and getting dressed is beyond daunting. Life in the ordinary is bizarre enough, but when you are ill it's like you are embroiled in a grand conspiracy, which you and only you will be able to bring to the light of day if you can just shake off your persecutors and unearth the clue that links these seemingly unrelated but, as you well know, far from fortuitous events, which you have divined as being at the heart of it all.

According to the mental health charity Mind, one in four people will experience some form of mental health problem each year, which means it has probably happened to someone close to you. Maybe you have experienced mental health problems yourself. I was diagnosed with Bipolar Affective Disorder, more commonly known as Manic Depression, in 2005 when I was eighteen years old. Bipolar is a serious and at times debilitating condition in which sufferers oscillate from extremes of depression and inertia to those of mania and hyperactivity. In its extreme form, Bipolar can even lead to psychosis, a state in which the sufferer loses touch with reality. Bipolar, according to Mind, will affect as many as 3 in 100 people during

their lifetime, a statistic that surprised me: even I
didn't realise how common my condition is. People
famously dislike talking about their mental
health. There is a stigma that hangs around these
issues. We absurdly carry our issues around
like some private shame and often avoid seeking
the support and treatment that could help us.
I want to give a clearer picture of what it means to
have a mental health condition. As inadequate
as the written word is, I want to provide a glimmer
of what it is like to live with an illness like this.

You can still be, at times, remarkably lucid and/or
functional. During one manic spell, I told the
ski company who were refusing to pay me overtime,
that I had fulfilled my contractual hours and that
they could take their group of sixteen, snotty,
unruly, over-privileged teenagers (four more than
the number of snotty, unruly, over-privileged
teenagers allowed by Swiss law) and teach them to
ski themselves. I managed to arrange and pack
my belongings, order coffees and pastries, charm
a Swiss family returning to Geneva in broken French
and buy tickets to travel (*merci monsieur, vous
avez une bonne après-midi*). I quite competently
made my way back, some 1155km, by means of
hiking, hitch-hiking, high speed train, coach and
Eurotunnel. I befriended a group of American
tourists staying at the same youth hostel and even
conducted a brief love affair with an Iranian artist
in Paris, before finally producing my papers
when prompted at the border without arousing any
suspicion to make it back to old Blighty.

Less than a week later I was institutionalised,
an incarceration that would last several months.

While it may not always be the case that you cannot
function and can appear to be well in control of
your faculties during these times, behind the eyes
your system of feedback is slowly corrupting,
your ability to interpret and respond to people and
events is working on a totally different loop to
the one occupied by others. This means that at
some point the information feeding back and forth
between you and others is going to miscompute.
At this point you are going to feel like a string of
sixes and eights in a binary system, and while you
recognise that you bear a relation to all those zeros
and ones, your values just won't correlate in any
meaningful sort of way. You are, as it were, a bug
in the system.

The most destructive thing about mental health
disorders is the way they move in self-fulfilling
cycles. Firstly you are fine and interact normally
with others. Then your perception becomes steadily
skewed and you start to act more eccentrically.
This eccentricity makes people look at you oddly or
become wary of you. When you notice this change
in attitude, you yourself become wary of how
other people are being, which in turn accentuates
your existing eccentricities. This goes on until
you find yourself in a paranoid state, unable to
interact with people in a functional way, ultimately
alienating yourself from those around you and vice
versa. And there is no greater boon to insecurity
than being alone.

There is an inevitable chain of events set in motion
when you end up in this paranoid state. You have
this clawing suspicion of anything and everything,
attributing significance to minor events or objects,

arbitrarily and spuriously. This suspicion wrings your heart with an anxiety that seems so acute as to be physically painful. It can become so severe that you feel like you want to pluck your heart out. You turn away from the outer world and begin to feel the problem inside you, internalising your obsession, interring your thoughts and turning your suspicion for the outside world in upon yourself.

Imagine then, with this anxiety and paranoia running through you that three or four burly men or policemen, fetch you out of your home, or pick you up off the street as may be the case, and bundle you into the back of a van (with varying degrees of force depending on how much you struggle). You are then taken to an unfamiliar clinical looking building where you are robbed of your shoe laces and belt or, at worst, all of your clothes altogether. In the latter case, you are dressed instead in a sort of apron with sleeves that leaves your backside exposed to a room full of strangers. You are then subjected to a physical assessment, which may include (but is not limited to), being poked and prodded, having your knee tapped with a rubber hammer, having things waved in front of your face, having a light shone in your eye and having your genitals rudimentarily inspected (though this may have been an eccentricity of the Canadian system in which I was once interred). You are then presented with some oddly coloured little pills which could be dragon' s teeth and told to swallow them on the proviso that if you don't there can be others found that will fit your anus.

You are then told that either a) you are sectioned under the Mental Health Act, which means you can't leave (whether you are in a fit state to understand this is immaterial), or b) that you are here of your own free will but that if you try to leave without the approval of a consultant psychiatrist you will be instantly sectioned (see above).

In the cold sober light of day these memories are unpleasant at best but when feeling vulnerable, anxious and paranoid they are tantamount to torture. They feed the paranoia. Like the man already far gone who feels compelled to drink more without really considering why and without having the cognitive faculties to know what's best for his health, you drink in this tide of events that only seem to affirm all your worst fears. As a result, you feel a great sense of vindication. You were right about them.

Things usually get a lot worse before they get any better.

There is the endless frustration and sterile boredom that oozes out of every inch of the beige walls, linoleum floor, tasteless meals and harm-proofed furnishing on what we euphemistically call a mental 'health' ward.

You are exempt from the law which applies to those deemed sane. You can be detained for an indeterminate length of time, deprived of possessions, forcibly medicated and in some cases violently electrocuted. This is still considered therapy in some institutions. Other countries go further and surgically remove large sections of the brain, even today. India I'm looking at you!

Despite the beginnings of a shift in the stigma surrounding mental health, there are many unhelpful stereotypes which permeate our culture today. Just the word 'psycho' produces a Hitchcock movie, or the chainsaw wielding, prostitute butchering Patrick Bateman of American Psycho. I have even been guilty of calling someone a psycho myself when they have acted unreasonably or irrationally. For some reason this sort of epithet seems to have remained socially acceptable to bandy about whilst it would raise eyebrows if someone were to refer to another as a 'spastic' owing to their physical ineptitudes. While there is certainly an ignorance of the distinction between psychosis and psychopathy, ultimately those who are mentally ill are more often a danger to themselves than they ever are to anyone else. They are more likely to be the victims of violent crime than they are to be the perpetrators.

So what do you do when you meet your real life psycho? We're all out there, working surreptitiously in secluded motels, playing the financial institutions of Wall Street, and yes, even writing in reputable Russell Group universities. Don't scream or run a mile, or kindle some form of primitive witch hunt. Say hi, go for coffee or a drink, catch a film, walk with a picnic to the top of Bole Hill with us, play Frisbee in the summer with us, have a snowball fight in the winter with us and take a hike to the Peaks in the spring with us. Treat me as you would anyone else you are building an acquaintance with, just appreciate that extra degree of difficulty it has taken for me to become your friend.

William Watts

Editors

Carmen Levick
Matilda Reith

Friday Tea Time, Sunday Dinner
(With apologies to
Ripping Yarns)

Characters:
REG, BERT and FRED (resentful proletarians). VERA (REG's wife)

SCENE ONE

REG and BERT walk slowly side by side and stop.

REG: ...they grind you down, chew you up and spit you out.
BERT: Tha' gets spat out.
REG: Then they sling you on the sodding scrapheap and expect you to be grateful for their pigging hand-outs.
BERT: The scrapheap, eh Reg?
REG and BERT start to walk again.
REG: They'll not consign me to the scrapheap, Bert.
BERT: They won't... I can see that.
REG: You'll not find me languishing on no scrapheap.
EXIT REG and BERT.
CURTAIN

SCENE TWO

REG is sitting on top of a tall pair of wooden stepladders; behind him a large painted sheet depicts an enormous heap of scrap, piled high with bits of metal sticking out at various angles and a sign reading BILLETS NON-FERROUS METALS.
BERT is walking along aimlessly, looking down at his feet, his hands in his pockets.

BERT: (looks up) Reg? Reg!
REG: Bert!
BERT: Reg! What happened brother?
REG: I only got thrown on the scrapheap, that's what.
BERT: But I thought... I mean how?

REG: A bloke came round with a clipboard Friday tea time and told me to get me cards.

BERT: A clipboard eh?

REG: Next thing I know, they've gone and thrown me on the sodding scrapheap.

BERT: After all you said as well.

REG: I know.

BERT: What will you do?

REG: Wait here, 'til someone comes and rescues me.

BERT: Good thinking, Reg.

BERT starts to walk off.

REG: Bert!

BERT: What?

REG: Aren't you going to rescue me?

BERT: Oh yeah... of course, brother.

REG: Well hurry up will you.

BERT: I'll go and get help.

REG: It's bloody murder is this, languishing on the scrapheap.

BERT sets off at a dash. He re-appears a moment later with FRED.

BERT: *(pointing at REG)* Look Fred, its Reg.

FRED: By the Christ, Reg. What happened?

REG: Can you not see what happened?

BERT: He's only gone and got himself thrown on the scrapheap, Fred.

FRED: Christ, that's bad.

REG: Are you going to get me down?

FRED and BERT help REG down. REG dusts himself off.

FRED: Are you alright, Reg?

REG: Course I'm not pigging alright. I've just been thrown on the scrapheap haven't I?

FRED: What will you do now Reg?

REG: Get even with the bastards, that's what.

FRED: I see.

REG: Scrapheap or no scrapheap. They'll not grind me down.

REG dusts himself down again.

REG: The bloody indignity of it.
REG EXITS. BERT and FRED follow him.
CURTAIN DOWN

SCENE THREE

REG, BERT and FRED are in a pub, each with a pint. They sit at a small round table, with six or seven empty bottles of beer on it. They are in sombre, reflective mood. There is a tense silence. Nothing is said. The men sip their pints. BERT consults his watch.

BERT: Blimey, it's gone 2pm.
REG: You what?
BERT: We've missed last orders.
REG: We've bloody missed last orders? Pigging hell, how did that happen?
BERT: Sorry Reg. It was my round as well.
REG: Can this day get any worse?
BERT: Not for you Reg, no.

REG, BERT and FRED all take a drink of their pint and put it down on the table at the same time. There is silence again.

BERT: Still... we've got 10 minutes drinking up time.
FRED: And a further 10 minutes to vacate the premises...
REG: Should the landlord choose to exercise his discretion in that regard.

They all take a drink of beer again in unison. There is silence.

BERT: Where did it all go wrong, eh?
FRED: You what?
BERT: Where did it all go wrong—that's what I want to know?
REG: I'll tell you where it all went bloody wrong.
BERT: Thanks Reg... I was hoping you might know.
REG: It was when we started getting fancy ideas, way above our station.
FRED: How do you mean?
REG: That was when it started to go wrong. Folk should have been happy with free prescriptions and Council housing, but no, they went and got all aspirational.
BERT: Aspiration's not for the likes of us.
REG: Over my dead body will I become aspirational.
BERT: Careful, Reg. Remember what happened when you said you wouldn't get thrown on the scrapheap?
REG: (gets to his feet, angry) Do you think I need pigging reminding, eh? Eh?
BERT: I were only thinking of your welfare.

REG: Well don't. Welfare's a dirty word round here.
REG sits down. The three of them each take a drink. There is silence.

BERT: You know who I blame?
Silence. No-one answers.

BERT: I said, do you know who I blame?
FRED: Go on, who?
BERT: The Tories.
FRED: The Tories?
BERT: Correct, the Tories.
REG: Don't talk to me about the bloody Tories.
FRED: How long have they been in power now?
BERT: Hmm... 35 years is it?
REG: (*bitterly*) 35 years eh? How the pigging hell did that happen?
FRED: We should never have got rid of Jim Callaghan.
REG: Don't talk to me about Jim Callaghan.
BERT: What's the matter with you Reg?
REG: Nothing's up with me, why?
BERT: We can't talk to you about the Tories. We can't talk to you about Jim Callaghan. We can't talk about the scrapheap...
REG having taken a drink of his beer, spurts some out. Wipes his mouth.
He gets to his feet, seething, and storms out.

FRED: Come on Bert sup up, you'll be late for your dinner.
BERT and FRED EXIT.
CURTAIN

SCENE FOUR

REG's wife VERA is at a stove with a frying pan. She wears a pinafore and headscarf and smokes an untipped cigarette. REG walks in, hangs his coat up, says nothing and sits down at the table.

VERA: You're home then?
REG: I am that.
VERA: And where have you been?

REG: I got thrown on the scrapheap if you really must know.

VERA: Ee, lovey.

VERA goes over to him, stands behind, puts her arm around his chest, goes to give him a kiss, but stands back before she does, noticing the smell of beer.

VERA: Funny sort of scrapheap was it?

REG: No. What do you mean? It was just a normal one.

VERA: I mean a scrapheap where they serve drink.

REG: It wasn't like that.

VERA: Weren't it?

REG: No. It were piggin' murder until Bert and Fred came and rescued me and took me to the pub.

VERA: Well yer dinner's ruined.

REG: He's a good mate is Bert, rescuing me like that.

VERA: Dinner's in the oven.

REG: I could still be languishing. Languishing on the scrapheap, if it wasn't for him.

VERA: Are you going to eat?

REG: Get it out for us would you love. I'm starving.

VERA goes over to the stove, dollops the burnt contents in frying pan on a plate. She goes over to the table carrying the plate with a few very badly burnt small items on it. She puts it down in front of him.

REG: It's burned.

VERA: I know.

REG: What the pigging hell is that?

VERA: Vol au vent and petit pois.

REG: What's wrong with pie and peas like we normally have?

VERA: It IS pie and peas, but in the French style.

REG: They're out of order them pigging French.

VERA: I'll chuck it in the bin then, you ungrateful sod.

REG: I'm expected to eat that for me Sunday dinner?

VERA: It were a decent enough size when it went in the oven.

VERA sits down at the table, opposite REG. He looks at his plate, moving the burnt pieces of food around with a fork.

VERA: Anyway, I've got some news.

REG: What have I said about aspiration? I might as well talk to me'self.

VERA: I'm going to have a baby.

REG: You wouldn't wish the scrapheap on... news?

VERA: Yes.

REG: What news?

VERA: I'm going to have a baby.

REG: You what?

VERA: Yes. A baby.

REG: No. NO!

VERA: Yes.

REG: (resigned) We'll bring him up proper.

VERA: Does it matter that it's not yours?

REG: How do you mean, not mine?

VERA: You're not the father.

REG gets to his feet, pushing the chair over behind him as he does.

REG: Well who in pigging hell's name is the father then?

VERA: It's Bert.

REG: What?

VERA: Bert, Bert, it's Bert's.

REG: Bert?

VERA: The... the two-faced get. Going behind my back like that. I'll bloody brain him for this.

VERA: Sorry Reg.

REG: First that business with him not warning me it was last orders. And now this.

VERA: It won't happen again.

REG: Too right it won't happen again, I'll not trust him to give advance warning of last orders again. Ever. He can forget it.

VERA: He rescued you from the scrapheap Reg, you told me yourself he did that.

REG: Can we not leave the scrapheap out of it?

REG grabs his coat and goes out of the door. VERA goes to the door, shouting after him.

VERA: Reg. Reg! How about we call the baby Bert, if it's a boy, I mean?

    CURTAIN.
    ENDS

Greg Challis

Editors

Paula Morris
Deepali Agarwal
Kathryn Blott
Greg Challis
Tamsin Connor
Katie Fisher
Katie Gadsby
Ethel Maqeda
Rachel McKinnie
Catriona McLean
Rebekah Rotherham

Home Soon

Winner of the 2014 Booker Prize Foundation Universities Initiative Short Story Prize

I was on the train the day of the bombs. Six hours waiting on the platform at St. Pancras, after a meeting I hadn't wanted to go to, for a job I didn't even like. Trains cancelled and delayed with no explanation; just text on a public announcement screen. Waiting on the draughty platform. Reading the notices about the need for the correct travel documentation and why you shouldn't leave your luggage unattended over and over again to pass the time; a crowd of other travellers restive around me. I suppose we all just wanted to get home. Then the tension electric when a train finally pulled in and the scramble to get on board. Doors closing too soon; a woman screaming on the platform. Falling into a miraculously empty seat and inadvertently meeting the glance of the woman opposite; blonde hair, startlingly green eyes replete with anguish. Her coloured contact lenses cannot veil her fear. Tapping out the text message to my husband: 'Made it. Train really late. Home soon. x.' Thinking about my husband as the train rattled north; about how I'd left him asleep in bed that morning.

It had still been dark, it had been so early. There had been a gap in the curtains and a band of orange from the street light outside had fallen across the duvet over his legs. How I hadn't wanted to go. How I was going to leave that job and stop having to make this journey for these pointless meetings once a week. How I should have resigned a long time ago now. How I'd left the children sleeping in their beds; how I should never have left them. A savage, almost visceral longing to be home, away from these strangers and off this train overriding all other senses. Then the train slowing, slowing before limping to a halt. A man with ragged black hair leaning over me, demanding, 'what station? Where are we?' Where are we? A quick glance out the window revealing nothing, a field. Could be anywhere. Nowhere. Then the boom in the distance; a tremor in the earth, the rattle of the windows. Where are we? Nowhere. With no place to go.

Why wait on the train after that? I suppose we didn't know what else to do. We could all see the darkening skyline. We all knew what it meant, and yet we didn't move. We were waiting for ... what? A conductor? A guard? Someone to check our travel documentation? Someone to tell us what to do next, now that everything we'd ever known was gone. Then someone did come. A soldier with a gun and a mask covering his face, herding us out into the field beside the tracks, like the sheep we were.

Then there were a lot of soldiers, using their rifles to prise open the doors to the train. The driver at the end of the train, expostulating with a soldier, gesticulating towards his train. The soldier raising his gun. A crack resounding in the air. The driver crumpling to his knees and bowing over before the soldier, his head resting upon the ground, as if overcome with melancholy. The man with the ragged black hair, leaning over me again and muttering into my ear, 'just do what they say.' Glancing up at him in surprise. It had never occurred to me not to.

Another soldier, this one with a red beret on and an air of importance; handing out masks and ordering us to put them on. Fumbling with it, almost gagging as it snapped around my face with the smell of burning rubber; too much like the Lapsang souchong tea the Director drank in the office. Being pushed inside a canvas-covered wagon and driven away. 'Where? Where to?' the man beside me is crooning to himself, rocking a little in his seat as if to comfort himself. I remember rocking the children when they were babies; the thought dances ruinously across my mind. Cradling their tiny backs with my hand, holding them close against my shoulder, joggling them up and down, up and down through the long nights when they wouldn't settle. The street light outside shining through the curtains into the nursery with a weak orange glow. Those nights when they had colic and cried all night and it felt as if I was the only person awake in the whole wide world. It doesn't matter where we're going. It's where we're not going that matters. We're not going home.

They take us to a centre. The centre is very clean and very white inside. The word pristine springs to mind. The army truck drives down a long dark tunnel to get to the light white centre. It is under-ground. They do not let us in until we have been decontaminated. It is not a pleasant process, but it cannot be helped. They do not want us to get dirt

into their clean white centre, like so many children's
fingerprints on glass, or crayon marks on a wall.
When we do eventually get inside, we discover the
centre is a warren of winding tunnels and seemingly
infinite rooms, like some vast country house
constructed underground. There will be servants'
quarters. There are always servants' quarters in
country houses, with walls painted yellow, perhaps,
to differentiate the servants' sections from
those of the flawless white masters'. They used to
stain the paint with urine. It is only a matter of
time before they get the measure of me, and send
me to the servants' quarters.

'This is the end,' they tell us. And then they add,
'but not the end.'

Make up your mind, I think.

'You are lucky,' they tell us. 'Lucky we found you
out there on that train. Lucky you got out of London
when you did. Lucky the train made it so close
to the shelter. Not many are so lucky. So many are
dead. Not just in London, but everywhere.'

Like the train driver, I think. Or my children.

'So many are dead, their bodies consumed by the
fire or the ash. Or if they are not dead now, they
will be soon. Dying of their injuries, or the diseases
which will inevitably come.' No one will clear up
their corpses. They will be left like so much rubbish
to rot in the streets. Their bodies will crumple into
themselves until they are as light as paper; blown
around by the winds, perhaps they will catch on
barbed wire fences like rags and shreds of plastic
bags. So much refuse left behind.

'You are lucky,' Dr Gerhardt tells us. 'This is the
end of the human race as it was, and yet, just the

beginning. Humanity can start again.' Dr Gerhardt's coat is as white as the walls and the floors. He knows how to make a new human race. This one will be better, he tells us. He's going to improve us; out of what's left he'll create something new. The next step in the evolutionary chain. He's going to plant this new human race in his test tubes and grow them in his laboratory. The first of them will grow up underground; of necessity, he tells us. The world outside is ruins and ashes, but one day, in the future, there will be sunlight again. He needs just a few pieces of all of us; the ones that remain. Just a few cells. There is a questionnaire, to find out what we are good at. He would be grateful if we could complete it. Then he will be pleased to examine us. He would like to see what features we have, ones to pass on which would be good for this new human race. I look around the assembled group. We are a mixture of soldiers, train passengers and a few other stragglers. Even though we are all clean and hosed and dressed in white, we are a shambolic bunch. I have my doubts.

'How do we know what's left outside?' the man with the ragged black hair demands. He has become belligerent as the days have passed. He is not taking his own advice; he is not just doing as they say. He wants to go home too. Dr Gerhardt blinks myopically at the man; analysing him from a distance. Nothing worth keeping there. The doctor nods infinitesimally at one of the guards who leads the man struggling away. Perhaps he will get to go home now, the man with the ragged black hair. Or perhaps, and more likely, like the train driver, he will soon be overcome with melancholy too.

148

I think about the sunlight that these new humans will see, when the world is as clean as the centre.

We will not get to see this sunlight. Sunlight shining through autumn leaves. Spring sunlight when the world seems fresh and newborn and green. Summer sunlight, parching the garden and making the roses blowsy. I don't miss the sunlight all that much. I miss the streetlight outside my house, shining like an orange beacon in the dark. How the sodium glow lit patterns in the pavement; they would spiral up to meet you as you walked. The certain knowledge that the dark house beyond was home, that everyone inside it was what mattered most.

Are my children really dead? Is my husband? I left him sleeping. Perhaps I think these thoughts a thousand times a day. Some days I don't think at all. It is better not to think. Dickens' Rachael shuffles into my mind, a bundle of Victorian shawls and skirts: 'Try to think not; and 'twill seem better.' It is good advice. I try not to think and things seem better. Poor Rachael working at her loom in the vast mechanised industrial north. It was a brave new world then too. Machines which could do the work of twenty men.

Look where they have brought us, these machines. Now we are weaving new life from the fabric of our DNA, or Dr Gerhardt is. I am not weaving anything. I am cleaning a kitchen surface. And then I am wiping tables; or emptying bins.

'We all must contribute,' Dr Gerhardt says.

'You must do what you can.'

He does not say what happens to those who don't; or those who can't. The trouble with my contribution is that the wiping of tables and emptying of bins gives one too much time to think.

It is a mindless occupation, cleaning. It is hard to follow Rachael's advice.

Dr Gerhardt doesn't want us to think too much either. 'What is there to reflect upon in the past?' he demands. 'Too many mistakes in the past. It's not good to be too sentimental.' So let's leave the past alone. The past is a foreign country to us now. Nostalgia is the original sin in our brave new world. We need to celebrate the future; of course we do. Celebrate the first produce from the laboratory. The new children containing bits and pieces of us all and some added magic from Dr Gerhardt's own recipe. Strange new children, with eyes of startling green. Not coloured contact lenses after all, then. Their skin isn't like baby's skin. It's soft, granted; but it's slippery too. No clammy handprints here.

Dr Gerhardt is determined to keep the new world clean. These children almost rustle as they move. Sleek, green eyed children, who grow too fast. They don't stay babies for long. Within a couple of days they are toddling. A week and they have a knowing look in their eyes, as if they know more than us. They stand in groups and observe us.

We are an anachronism already. They almost reach to my shoulder, like my eldest son on his eleventh birthday. He was almost taller than me then. Tall and skinny, bony elbows and knees; long legs he didn't quite know what to do with. Awkward like a newborn foal. Curled up in his bed when I left that morning. He would have got up and gone to school; and then … Well, I'll never know now. If I'd known, I would have kissed his sleeping head as

I'd left. *If I'd known, I'd never have left at all.* One of them sidles up to me as I'm wiping over the tables in their quarters. He holds something black in his hand.

'Who is "x"?'

I stop wiping tables and bend down to him, suppressing a shudder as I do so. I cannot help it, even though it is just a child. This child is not like my eldest son.

'What's that?' I ask. He has my mobile phone. The screen is open on the sent messages. Made it. Train really late. Home soon. x.

'I'm surprised that still works.' I laugh a little, and then stop. It sounds too much like choking.

'Did you find a charger for it?'

'Who is "x"?' the child demands again. They are nothing if not utilitarian. They are Gradgrind and Bounderby. They want facts.

'I am.' I smile and force myself to stroke the child's ragged black hair. Perhaps there was something worth keeping after all. 'I am x. The last letters in the alphabet. The last of us.'

The child smiles and nods as if this makes sense, as if I have given the correct answer. When he smiles he seems more human. More like my son. He moves closer to me still, and this time it doesn't seem so strange.

'Tell me about the old world,' the child insists.

I put my cleaning cloth down and sit down at the table I have been wiping. He sits down beside me.

'I was on the train,' I say, 'the day of the bombs.'

Val Derbyshire

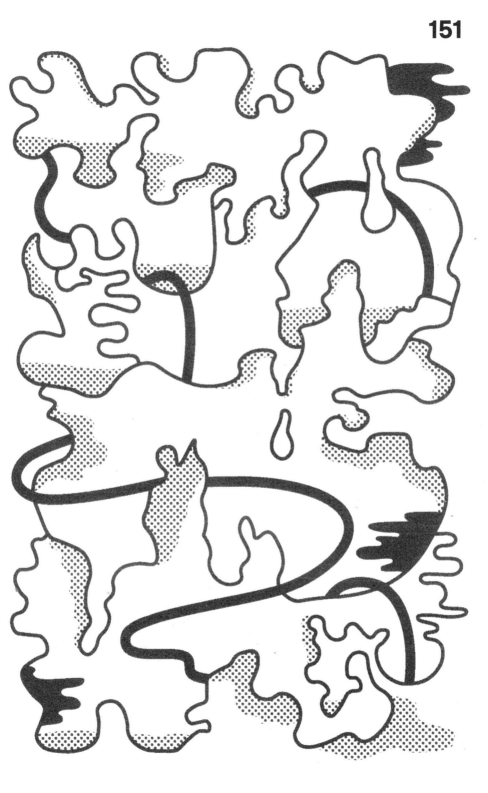

The Gull

'What's that?'

The question lodged itself in Lee's mind, its context lost within a Rorschach image of white and grey. A vehicle, a building and a group of men, all viewed from above and reduced to a collection of monochrome shapes. Orders are given, repeated and carried out. Then comes the question — 'What's that?' — and the shapes are gone.

On the flight back to New York he continued to replay the operation in his head, but tens of similar, half-forgotten scenarios blurred into one another, white shapes shifting and changing, running together. The only image that stood out in the mess was that of his colleague's face. No matter how well an operation had gone, Joel would always be wearing the same calm expression: no praise for a job well done, but no condemnation when things went sideways either. This time, he had seemed shocked, even haunted. By the time the plane touched down, the only other memory he'd recovered was of the sudden tug at his gut when all those shapes had disappeared.

When Lee was finally back in the familiar surroundings of his home and the comfort of his own bed, he started having the dream. In it, he lies on his back gazing up at the blazing sun, sand hot against his bare skin, between his toes and fingers. Dunes surround him, waving like ocean tides, blown by winds he can't feel or hear. Nothing happens for a long time. Eventually, a white gull appears, flying low overhead until it blots out the sun. Then he wakes up. That's it.

There are variations. Sometimes he wakes before the gull comes into view, the knowledge that it will eventually arrive having the same effect as its actual appearance, a dread he can't put into words. Sometimes he starts to dream something completely different, only for his surroundings to crumble around him until he is once more lying in sand and staring up at the sun.

Lee spent many hours thinking about this dream, but to rob it of meaning rather than to ascribe it: to dissect it, break it down into its constituent parts and identify them. He thought that if he did this, maybe he could break the spell, stop waking with a start in the small hours of the morning and disturbing his wife, Samantha, with a loud gasp. After much deliberation, he decided that the vivid feeling of hot sand might come from days spent lazing on the beach on childhood vacations. Perhaps that one year they flew to Santa Barbara when he was fifteen, and he had gone to watch girls playing volleyball, only to fall asleep on the sand and wake up burnt, lobster pink. But Lee knew that he was only fooling himself, stretching for the wrong answers, and he soon gave up on all attempts at analysis.

Instead, in an effort to distract himself, he has taken to reading more. Usually he takes one of Samantha's volumes on history or architecture, but sometimes he stops off at a book store, browsing the shelves until something catches his eye — the search for a distraction being an equally effective distraction in itself. If he should happen to find himself without a book to hand, he will read whatever is lying around — pamphlets, magazines, it doesn't matter. He reads until his eyes become hooked on a line or paragraph, skipping like a stuck record, the words becoming indecipherable marks on the page. Today Lee is reading one of his wife's books: a drawn-out analysis of Brutalist architecture in Europe by a J. Blackstock. He closes it and rubs his eyes to wipe away the few words that remain, swimming in his vision.

The old television set in the corner flickers with washed-out images. A bearded man in a life vest is talking about trout but his gruff voice is reduced to a tinny whine by the speakers. Lee's father sits in a threadbare armchair, eyes fixed on the screen. He hasn't said a word for hours. That's all right, though: Lee isn't here for the conversation, he's here for the white noise. He's here because the place is filled with enough light distractions that he can't fall into the well of his own thoughts. He's here because everything in this building is at the halfway mark. Everything is either 'not quite' or 'slightly'. The walls are not quite white. The rooms smell slightly of disinfectant. At lunchtime, he watched one of the carers bring in a tray of something halfway between baby food and a steak dinner and place it on the table by his father.

At first, the choice of retirement home had been the source of many bitter arguments between Lee and his sister, Janice. She had made the arrangements while Lee was on the other side of the globe, placing their father in a small facility just outside of Berwick, Pennsylvania. He insisted that their father always wanted to remain in New York City, but his protests fell on deaf ears, and besides, it was done: contracts had been signed and money had changed hands. Four years older than Lee, she claimed that she knew better than her baby brother, and that it was the best they could afford, though how she could come up with the money working as a receptionist at JFK was a mystery to him.

It was despite himself, then, that Lee found that he enjoyed, even anticipated, the long drive west along the interstate. Once out of New York's traffic tangle, there was nothing but rolling green for miles and the steady sound of forward motion. This chance to switch off everything but autopilot had become half the reason his visits to his father had been increasing. It had been after this discovery that Lee had written himself the schedule: a list of distractions which he followed to the letter. Despite having memorised the whole list, he keeps it in his pocket, just in case he is ever without something to read. Today is Wednesday.

```
until    0700: read
0700 - 0715: breakfast
0715 - 0745: newspaper
0745 - 0800: small chores
0800 - 1100: Berwick
1100 - 1800: dad, lunch
1800 - 2100: home
2100 - 2200: dinner, read
```

Today, though, it hadn't worked. His mind had been racing since the moment he woke, a relentless spinning newsreel that outpaced the car along the interstate. The book hadn't helped either. He hadn't even read it, just stared at its contents until a meaningless black scrawl was emblazoned on his aching eyeballs. The white noise and the beige middle-ground of the nursing home had lost their magic. Last night, the gull never came.

That morning, he had woken slowly, naturally, and to bright sunlight rather than the dim opening act of a new day. The clock's glowing screen read 8:23am. Yet there had been no comfort in this, the first truly restful sleep he'd had in weeks, nor had there been any comfort to be found in his morning routine, performed automatically, something he usually relied on to wipe away whatever ghosts of the dream remained. That there had been no dream was the least comforting thing of all.

Downstairs, Samantha was waiting, breakfast on the table — a job that, up until then, Lee had been taking care of in his attempt to accumulate as many small distractions as possible.

'Good morning,' she said with a smile, and poured him a cup of coffee. 'Those sessions must be having an effect. I haven't seen you looking so rested in a long time.'

'Yeah,' Lee replied, returning what he hoped was a convincing smile.'I guess Hopper really is as good as he claims.'

After many nights of disturbed sleep, Samantha had tried to persuade Lee to see a therapist. Eventually he acquiesced and made an appointment with a military psychologist, despite the fear that he would get sucked back into another cycle of trying and failing to remember, and end up breaking the routine of distractions that had started to serve him so well.

The office was a drab, government funded box, and the psychologist, a Sergeant John Hopper, looked uncomfortable in his fatigues, like a highschool geography teacher longing for a knitted sweater. Despite Lee's initial misgivings, and after being told, in no uncertain terms, that he should have been to see him sooner, Hopper seemed friendly and understanding. He talked at length about the importance of giving voice and order to the events that troubled Lee, encouraging him to start from the beginning and continue at his own pace. Lee had tried to do as the psychologist requested, giving an account of an operation he was increasingly convinced was jumbled up with tens of similar jobs, and attempting to put words to the gap in his memory, but each attempt fell short.

Each time, either the account would ring false, the jigsaw pieces of the operation never quite fitting together, or he would fail to convey how heavily those absent details weighed on his mind. It didn't help that he felt the need to edit everything he said, so as to not look incompetent or unstable, just in case any of the notes Hopper was constantly taking should make it into some job suitability assessment or other. After a second session, during which Lee continued to trip over his own thoughts and words, he was beginning to think therapy was a waste of time.

He never kept his third appointment. His doubts and misgivings had stopped him in his tracks as he stared at Hopper's name, sitting in its brown plastic sheath on the plain, grey-painted door, his hand hovering over the handle. Instead, he turned around, marched back through the small waiting room and read in a coffee bar until an appropriate amount of time had passed, at which point he went home. That night, he gave Samantha a vague but believable summary of the session and let her think he would keep attending them regularly. He even wrote the appointments into his schedules for Monday and Friday, should she happen to find them folded up in his jacket pocket.

Lee had been surprised at how easy the deception had been to maintain, how naturally he could apply the careful limiting of information that his job required of him to all the non-classified goings on of his daily life. It didn't stop him feeling terrible whenever vagueness wouldn't do and outright lies were required though. At least Samantha didn't seem too bothered by his frequent absences. Sometimes he thought she didn't notice, guessing her job as an architect kept her busy. She was always scrutinizing some blueprint or other by the time he was out the door, and usually still working by the time he returned. With the Air Force sending him across the globe for months at a time, it probably wasn't much of an adjustment for her to make. That was the way their lives seemed to be structured.

'What's that?'

The question floats back as Lee stares at the television. The man in the life vest has finished talking about trout and is now riding in the back of a truck laden with fishing tackle, the whine of his voice barely audible over the engine; a noise that the TV's old speakers translate as newspaper being crumpled. There had been a truck, back then, on the other screen. A battered heap covered in a sheet, dents and patches of rust obvious even through thermal imaging. It had driven for miles along dirt roads until it had entered the frame of Lee's monitor and pulled up outside the compound. Men disembarked and others exited the building, bright white shapes shuffling around in a monochrome world. There was an exchange of acknowledgements. He rattled off coordinates, targets, confirmations into his headset and to Joel, sitting beside him, whose eyes were fixed on his own screen, finger hovering over the trigger.

This sudden burst of images, at last in some kind of logical order, prompts Lee to pull the Wednesday list out of his pocket and snatch up a pencil that had been discarded by an untouched book of cross-word puzzles — left there, he suspects, by his sister. On the back of the list, he begins to draw. A rectangle for the compound. Another for the truck. Soon he is looking at a series of angles and perimeters, a crude set of blueprints. Nothing that would impress Samantha, but it will suffice. Next he draws the men, pencilling in circles where their white shapes would have been. Two by the south entrance, another by the east. Three to unload the truck. The driver and two passengers. There were more, but the memory is degrading again, the monitor's contents lost to a tide of static.

Lee scrunches the piece of paper into a ball, letting it drop noiselessly onto the beige carpet, and rubs his eyes once more. When he looks up again, his father is studying him, the fishing lecture from the man in the life vest no longer able to hold his attention. Lee picks up the balled-up note and returns it to his pocket.

'Just work stuff,' he says. His father looks him up and down with a critical eye.

'I always said you should never have joined the force.'

'I don't remember you ever saying that.'

Lee has sat with his father for many hours over the course of several weeks, but this is the first time he's heard anything out of him that wasn't a complaint about the food or the staff.

'Janice says so too. She says they messed you up.'

'Does she now,' says Lee.

Samantha had invited Janice over for dinner one night, just before he started seeing Hopper, despite knowing that Lee and his sister don't get along. Lee had found the night strange — how the two women had seemed to conspire together, steering the conversation as if trying to get something out of him without actually asking. He had gone to bed early with a headache, leaving them in the dining room and his meal half finished.

Lee thinks of Joel, as he had done many times before — times when he had reached for his phone, hoping for some reassurance from his colleague, only to remember his face after that last operation. But today that memory isn't enough to make him pause and reconsider. He pulls the phone from his pocket to find it switched off, its black screen dead, and when it blinks into life he discovers there is very little charge left in the battery — just enough to scroll through a long list of missed calls and messages. Samantha, Joel, and even Janice appear on the list, each of their names flashing past multiple times. Of the numbers with no names attached, Lee recognises several belonging to the Air Force. Confused, Lee turns it off before the charge drains completely. He opens the door, the plainness of which reminds him of Sergeant Hopper's, and mumbles that he'll be back in a minute. His father's questioning stare follows him until he's out of sight.

The corridor is a length of mundane drabness that promises the same around the corner, and the next, zigzagging off into a beige, vaguely hospital-like infinity. Lee walks, wondering how such oppressively sanitised nothingness could ever have distracted him from the unfinished black-and-white movie now playing on a loop in his head. He walks until he finds his way through the beige labyrinth and reaches the entrance, with its row of payphones.

Lee empties his pockets of change, pushes some into the coin slot of the nearest phone and dials Joel's number. As he waits, he notices the plastic surfaces of the phones, their grime standing out against the stiflingly immaculate surroundings. There's a click.

'Hello?'

'Joel?'

'Is that you, Lee?'

'Yeah, I'm —'

'Where the hell have you been?' asks Joel, his voice raised in a stifled half-shout. 'Haven't you been getting the messages?'

'I only just switched my phone on.'

'You can't just stop showing up, you have to report in. Your leave ended days ago.'

'What?'

'Look, Lee, a psychologist, Hopper, phoned yesterday,' says Joel, his voice softening. 'I know the last one was difficult. If something is wrong, you're not going to get into trouble over this, just as long as you come in.'

The more Joel speaks, the more Lee involuntarily draws back his hand, so that, by the time he pauses to think, he finds the handset several inches from his ear, with Joel's voice becoming much like that of the man in the life vest. The words are going in, but they aren't making any sense. It's true that he hasn't been keeping track of time beyond the daily lists of tasks he has written for himself, but surely not so much that he would forget to report for duty.

'What happened?' asks Lee.

'I just told you, they need you to report in.'

'No, the last operation.'

'I don't know, you said you saw something. You stared at that monitor for ages. I had to take you out of the room myself.' Joel sighs. 'We really shouldn't be speaking about this on the phone.'

The words continue to sound hollow. He would have remembered something like that.

'What did I see?'

'Come on, Lee.'

'Please.'

There is a long pause. Lee can hear Joel's feet, shuffling in place, followed by another sigh.

'You said there was a kid in the back of the truck.' Another pause. 'But I didn't see anything, and they let me view the recording. It's not in any of the reports.'

Lee isn't listening anymore. He's staring at the receiver and the men are leaving the truck, white

shapes moving to the back, unloading boxes.
They are soon joined by more, moving out of the
compound, guns slung over their shoulders.
One remains motionless, another white shape
vis-ible through the truck's sheet covering. As the
men move towards the compound with their cargo,
Lee advises the strike. The confirmation comes
over his headset. A nod to Joel and the warhead is
away. Only then, in those dead seconds between
launch and impact, before thirteen pounds of
explosives puts an end to the scene playing out on
Lee's monitor, does the white shape in the back
of the truck stir. A smaller shape breaks away from
the larger, like a cell dividing under a microscope.
Lee watches the way it moves. It's not like the other
shapes.
     'What's that?'

Light slanted through the vast hangar doors,
rendering the white of the outstretched wings even
whiter. It was the first time Lee had seen a drone
up close. Before they started generating a mass of
negative press, the Air Force had been inundated
with applications from the lower ranks, a great deal
of whom saw it as a safer career path than many
the service had to offer. Lee was no different. He
had a wife to think about, after all. And what if
they started a family? At least sitting at a monitor
would ensure he came home in one piece.
     A bunch of those who made it past the aptitude
test crowded around the gleaming Predator and
listened to the Sergeant list its specifications. Lee
didn't think the name fitting. It didn't look much like
a 'predator', but more like a seagull, or perhaps an
albatross.

Peter S Dorey

Ratland

'Go back to Ratland Rat!'

Adiz scampered away. He checked behind to see
if the big man was chasing him, fear catching in his
throat. The big man wasn't; he had already turned
his back and unsteadily wandered up the crowded

street. Cowering in a yellow tiled doorway, Adiz breathed deeply and tried to ignore the curious shoppers.

Adiz Kamper was not, in fact, a Rat. He was a Mouse. From his whiskers to his tail it was obvious, and sometimes painfully obvious, that he was a five-foot-six, thinly furred, increasingly gaunt Mouse. But the Humans still called him Rat, as they called Rema, a pot-bellied and excessively loud Cockroach, a Rat. They were all the same in Humanitaria.

He kept breathing heavily, attempting to control the ensuing panic attack. It was the way the big man had slapped his paw that brought this on. He was only trying to examine the strange foreign currency more closely; the colours and sizes were all so confusing. All Adiz wanted was the cake advertised in the window, but a hand slapped on top of his and suddenly, Adiz was back in Mouseonia. That was how they first arrested him. He held up his paw in a handshake and the official in sunglasses smacked it down as if he were holding a knife. He still remembered the sting sometimes. The next blow, to his head, left a scar.

Adiz slowly came to breathe normally. The curiosity deadened, people's eyes rolled from him to the display window, their arms straining with the weight of bulging plastic bags, like trees drooping with over-ripe fruit. The shop was bursting full of plasma screen televisions, over-sized speakers, mobiles and tablets, twinkling and reflecting in the glare of lights that transformed the walls into a planetarium. A disgruntled store-assistant was coming over to the doorway. Heaving himself up, and keeping his head bowed and shoulders hunched, Adiz began to scurry home. The unspent change jingled in the pocket of his tracksuit with every step. It was probably best he didn't buy that cake; it would have cost him a meal tonight. But sometimes you miss the simple pleasures. Adiz shook his head, dismissing the thought as if it were an irritating fly, and scurried faster.

The city started to transform around him, from the smooth, clean metal of the city centre, to the more decrepit high office blocks, green smudges under every old window. His accommodation was beyond that, a council house crammed against its neighbours, built in a cheery, utopian vision of societal companionship. The greying bricks and littered gardens spoilt this dream, encouraging the residents to be as bleak and as cold to each other as the street was to them.

Adiz had moved in just under a fortnight ago. The nice Human from the charity had organised it. With no common language between them she had communicated with smiles and gestures that this was his home now. Home. That word, at least, came through. Adiz tried his best to repeat it in Human, but his natural Mouseonian squeak dominated his lips. Home. How could anyone call this a home? His room was tiny, the door not opening all the way before hitting the bed, the bed squeezed next to the wardrobe, the wardrobe only opening a slither before knocking the desk. The ceiling looked like it had been hastily repaired several times, cracks traced along it like lines on a map, the walls were softly crumbling at every corner, dampness soaking through methodically every winter.

No air-freshener could overpower the stench of a rotting house mixed with the sweat of too many individuals residing within its corpse, for there were

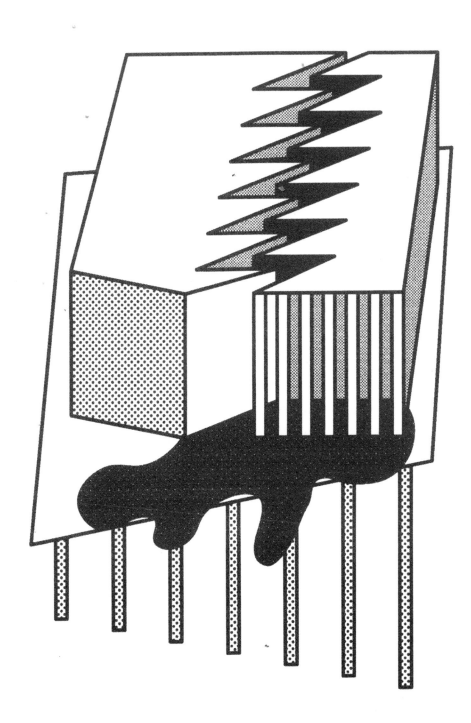

several residents, and every one of them in a room like Adiz's. Rema had been there longest, his belly large and his legs weak, so he often sat rather than stood. But his experience of living in Humanitaria held authority over the others, who orbited around his portly gravity. Samba was an Ant, he had only just turned nineteen and lived in Rema's shadow, following him wherever he went, and being the only appreciative audience to Rema's ramblings. He had a particular twitching habit with his neck, jerking his head from side to side. There were others, but Adiz had not yet learnt who they were, or even if they lived with him or just came visiting.

As he pushed his way through the stiff front door Adiz always liked to stop, close his eyes, and picture entering his real home, in Mouseonia. The scent of surrounding pine filtered into the house with every breeze. The hallway was wide and tall, pictures smiling down from nearly every space, his children, at different ages and in different places, his old Mama at the park, weddings and parties and dinners. His wife, Venesee, would play the radio softly in the kitchen, but loud enough that Adiz would try and sneak in unheard to surprise her with a tickle, which made her snigger. That joke lost its humour after a while. Eventually she would simply lay in their bed all day, one eye glued to the T.V, the other on the door, waiting for his return. He always saw her before she saw him. She would look haggard and sickly, and then he entered the room and she allowed a weak smile to ripple across her face.

'Why do you do it every day Adiz? Why?' she would sometimes ask, when the children were put to bed.

'You know why, my love.'

'Is it worth it? Is it worth it for our family's safety?'

Adiz always responded to this with a sigh.
He sighed now, opening his eyes to gloom and
dampness in every corner, to smell the wafts
of mould, to push the door closed and fumble with
lock after lock after lock. It wasn't worth it.

Rema had saved up enough to buy meat. He said he
had been putting a pound aside every week for
the past month and had his eye on a juicy chicken
breast.

'And juicy it is too, just like my old ladies breast,
ha!' Rema thumped one of his six massive legs on
the table. Samba swung his own leg onto the table
and laughed quietly. North Cockroach neighboured
Mouseonia, so Rema used a bastardised form
of Mouse, for Adiz's benefit. In particular Rema had
trouble with the last part of Adiz's name, instead
pronouncing it with an 's' and a shower of spittle.

'Yes you look like you need good meal, Adiss!'
Rema had shared the lunch between the three of
them: a steaming bowl of stock and scant meat.

'It's good, ay?'

Food often dominated the conversation in their
house; Rema took great pleasure in dishing out
both advice and snacks. His breakfast would often
consist of watery porridge, and for lunch some
plain rice, a diet he called 'a King's pittance', though
Adiz wondered whether he knew what this actually
meant.

'Yes, it's lovely, thank you.'

Samba nodded his head appreciatively which
immediately sent his neck into a spasm, stopping
only when he clutched his throat.

'This chicken travels almost as far as we did, ay!
Look, look, "free range from Chickenany,"' he said,

reading from the packet. 'Free range! I bet life is nice as chicken, ay, all space they want, all food they want! Though, if I chicken, I would have to be a chicken cannibal, ha!'

Adiz nodded his head.

'What you do today Adiss? I thought you went town to find job? Though you know you not allowed, crazy cheese eater!'

Adiz had gone to town that morning in the vague hope of applying for a job. It was after another evening where his dinner had consisted of the smallest and meanest vegetables he could find. The hours preceding it had been spent in a haze of wandering the city and, in the morning, trying to read the little squiggles that formed Human language, his duvet wrapped around him for some protection against the elements that his home was supposed to block out. But he went knowing that his courage would fail. It was illegal for him to get a job; they would deport him. So he had scurried up and down the high street, until his eyes had found the cake.

'No I — I didn't think it was a good idea in the end.'

'I know because I say is not! You mice all same, you have big ears, but for what purpose? Ha!'

Samba chuckled.

'You have to sign on later yes?'

Adiz nodded.

'Yes, it not good! But soon will be every six months rather than every week, ay.'

'It's really not so bad Adiz.' Samba looked up at the ceiling and his voice was barely a whisper. 'You just have to sign your name and then you're out of there.'

Adiz nodded again. He had been dreading this. The angry man had told him about it. Without looking at Adiz, or the interpreter, he had spoken to the folder in front of him, saying that Adiz would need to sign on at the government building every week, just so they knew where he was. In fact he had said a lot, all in one continuous monologue. When Adiz had tried to ask him questions at the end the man hadn't even listened before he threw the folder aside and, with a jerk of his coffee cup, indicated the door.

'I could... I could go with you? That is, if you like?' Samba politely inquired to the hanging light bulb.

'No, I'm sure it'll be fine. Thank you though, Samba.'

'Yes I remember first time I go there.' Rema gnawed on a chicken wing. 'You know North Cockroach was owned by the Humans? That's why my Human is good, ay. I remember going into that building and thinking: 'they will help me, they used help my country, no?' But no, they not help — when I ask, women say: 'who do you think you are?' They leave me living like this for two years! I sleep on street until I got this room. You know what I said to Samba here? I said it's going back to the whip. It's going back to them, just so they whip you all over again, yes?'

Adiz nodded his head automatically, having heard this story before. He mimicked looking at his watch, which had stopped working several months ago. Samba and Rema wished him goodluck and Samba came to lock him out.

'Don't mind him, Adiz.' Samba spoke to his feet. 'I haven't told you yet but I — I was in a detention centre. You know what that is, right? Good. Just know that — that anything here is better than anything there.' He looked up. 'This is screwed up. But just play by the rules, and you can get by.'

He closed the door softly into Adiz's perplexed face. He knew what happened in detention centres. He had heard enough about it on his journey here. A bony and chattering Mouse had told him all about it as they squashed into the boat together, their knees pushed painfully close. He told Adiz how he had reached Humanitaria before, and was arrested. They put him into the detention centre where the guards screamed at him; where a boy and fellow Mouse, not even eighteen, was put in the cell with him and had cried for his mother every night. 'What rule did I break?' He would ask, his face uncomfortably close, eyes questioning, 'I was a prisoner but committed no crime!'

Adiz started scampering because the government building was in the middle of the office blocks. He had no idea that Samba had been in such a place but it made sense now. No one in that house could be called healthy. At night their house felt like an asylum: screams, or at best mutterings, emanated from every room. His dreams were often of the day he left, the image of a door crooked on its hinges, of glass sprinkled across the wide corridor, glittering like a frozen sea, and what was upstairs ... When he awoke several times a night, he heard Samba's muffled sobs and Rema going into his room with soothing tones. But he had never imagined he had gone through that.

He approached the door of a gravel-coated building, the archway was endowed with the biggest green smudge of any of its neighbours, suspended in mid trickle. Adiz could see the queue to the desk and its mismatched and shuffling people.

How did things get so bad?

A man pushed past him, eyes focused on his phone. Looking over his shoulder to observe the obstacle,

connecting Adiz with the building he breathed
the first word Adiz had understood in Human: 'Rat.'

'Mouse!' Adiz put his hand to his mouth. He
couldn't quite believe he had said it.

The man, dressed in a blue suit and tie, had heard.
Without moving closer, he turned to fully face Adiz.
His angry face spat out words which Adiz didn't
understand. There was a pause after he had finished,
waiting for a reply.

'I ... Mouse.' Adiz said in his best Human. The man
moved closer. Adiz held his ground but shrank. His
chest constricted.

He said more words at more speed, and an
accusing finger came up, jabbing in his direction
like a dagger. Adiz could see the darkened rings
under his eyes and hair displaced from his groomed
scalp. He held up both paws and began to stammer.
'I — home, home!' His breath was short. The man
bellowed this word back at him, and screamed
more. Adiz understood some.

'Home?' 'No!' 'Rat.' 'Rat.' 'Rat!'

'Stay quiet.' A deep, accented, Mouseonian
voice muttered in his ear. A thin, brown Rat slipped
in front of him, placing himself between Adiz and
the man.

He said some words quietly in Human. The man
continued to shout, but the Rat never shouted back,
brushing the screams away with slow paw
movements and tilting his head to one side as he
listened. The man quietened. After a few more
words he threw up a hand in frustration, like waving
a flag, and stalked off. The Rat turned to Adiz.

'Are you all right, my friend?'

'Yes I — I think so, I, thank you.' He put a paw
to his chest, lungs loosening. He straightened up
properly.

'Don't worry. The name's Terez.' He gave a warming smile and extended a thin paw. 'Come. Let's get a coffee.'

'I — I can't, I need to sign.'

His dark eyes drank him in. 'You can sign later, come for coffee now. It's only round the corner.'

Without another word he led Adiz on around the corner to a grubby looking church. It was made from old stone that was weathered and rough, but looked like it was cowering in fear from the tall surroundings. They went through the doors to a wooden floored hall, bustling with Beetles, Cockroaches, Ants, Rats, Humans, even a few Badgers, sitting around tables drinking tea. They all laughed and talked, the person speaking never interrupted, the star of the table until another wanted to speak.

'Your first time here?' Terez handed him a coffee and guided him to an abandoned table. Several people shouted greetings at him and he waved back.

'Yes, what is this place?'

'Speak society. Some come to improve their Human, some come to talk in their own tongue.' Adiz nodded appreciatively and looked around once more.

'How long have you been here, my friend?'

'Longer than I'd like.'

He looked at Adiz keenly. 'Do not worry about what happened. It happens to us all. It ... it is not easy to live here.'

He described his trip to Humanitaria. The smugglers not telling him where he was going, forcing him into the dark, the immobilising space he was kept in, the man who unwittingly released him, shouting and kicking him. Terez ran, and spent most of his first month on the street. Eventually, finding the authorities, he was told he should have reported as soon as he got here. As if he even knew which country he was in.

'This is a strange new world we're in,' he muttered.

Adiz clutched his mug. 'It's a cruel world. Why don't they see? How can they live with the way we live?'

Sombrely, he studied the room.

'They choose to see us as different; they choose to treat us as different. You see, they are... forgetful when they want to be. They forget what sort of society they created, forget why they created it. They're proud of their history, but they're cursing it with this present.'

Adiz looked at his watch and jumped up, pointing out he must sign, but would come back. Terez nodded gracefully and clasped his paw again.

Adiz scuttled out of the church and returned to the busy shopping centre. He went back to the shop he had cowered in front of this morning, an electric sun now in the growing gloom, and stood outside. There were women inspecting screens, seeing the T.V but not the news, kids jostling and scrambling over each-other to play the latest consoles, men in black suits, their hands behind their back, necks rotating. He closed his eyes for a minute. The jabbering of the shoppers, the speakers buzzing, the T.V's roaring melded together and became louder and louder, forming a howl, echoing up to the lonely half-moon that silently gazed upon the earth. Adiz opened his eyes and straightened up. He walked towards the government building to sign his name, to say that he was a destitute Asylum Seeker, to say he was still here.

Nick Gore

Dinosaur Soup

Dr. Maloney,
I think you should take a look at what Matthew has been producing in the writing circle. He is really starting to worry me. Such an intense individual.

Finch

From Matthew's journal—

Week 1 — Setting
The shed stood alone at the bottom of the garden. Patches of paint had worn off to reveal the original, cheap pine of the thing. The door was difficult to open, so a spade and a pair of long-handled shears leaned outside it. The combination lock was stiff for lack of handling. Inside, it shared the universal smell of sheds everywhere; compost and rotting wood with a petrochemical undertone. A lawnmower languished in the corner, the workbench was

crowded with terracotta plant pots and gardening gloves, unworn since father left. Under the bench was a canister of petroleum for the lawnmower.

The Bloomfield Institution was a high-security mental hospital. From the outside it looked like a country house: picturesque aged brickwork and a garden out back, with benches scattered around for patients to sit on and gawp at the roses. High fences all around it, spikes pointing inward. Inside, the place had been gutted and repainted white, which was calming, and a muted green meant to be calming but actually nauseating. The patients' rooms were furnished nicely enough: some of us had carpets and patterned curtains. On the chipboard table next to my bed sat two mediocre books by Joshua Finch and a battered Bible. They put the Bible in there to give the patients Solace in the Word of God. Eventually we got bored enough to read it, but it didn't really have any effect.

Week 2 — Character
The boy was ten-and-a-half. We will call him David and not Matthew. Josh Finch says that this is fiction and it can be about anyone and anything I want it to be, and that I should not dwell on things. The boy wore a dressing gown over a pair of pyjamas that were not warm enough for outside. Adults always said that he looked half starved, but he explained to them that he just wasn't hungry. He did not think of himself as rebellious or anti-authoritarian by nature (and would not have done even if he had known the word 'anti-authoritarian'); he had just been finding it difficult to concentrate for the last year or so.

He would buck up eventually and land a job doing data entry for an office supply company called StapleMate. But back then, the teacher would have to say his name three times to drag his attention from the window to ask him a question, which he wouldn't understand. This confused him. It made him anxious and even less likely to pay attention. Apart from that day's lesson — he paid attention then because it was about dinosaurs, at least indirectly, and he loved dinosaurs.

Thoughts in His Head — He had learned in school how natural oil was created, how it was made up of dead things like algae and fish and dinosaurs, billions of years ago. They would die and sink to the bottom of the ocean, and then heat and pressure and time would turn them into a liquid. The liquid could be pumped out of the ground and made into all kinds of useful things, like petrol and diesel and plastic. This meant that toy dinosaurs were made out of real dinosaurs, and that his Mother's car ran on dinosaur soup.

'Mother' is spelled with a capital to show that she is an imposing figure who loomed large in David's mind. Mother was thin too, all elbows and cheekbones and crow's feet at the corners of her eyes. Mother always took care of her little boy, but had been finding it difficult to keep track of him recently and was more prone to shouting. The number of people in her house had changed but the number of wine bottles stayed the same.

Joshua Finch was a small man in early middle-age who had begun to sag around the edges. His hair melted from his head, starting at the crown and working outwards: when he turned around the light would glint off it. He insisted that all of the circle call him 'Josh' because this helps to build rapport. He genuinely believed in the power of writing to 'heal the mind and order the soul', as he put it. If you stared at him hard he sweated as though you had heat-beam eyes like Superman.

Week 3 — Action

It was too early and too cold to be awake, but David had a mission. He was Being a Scientist. He was Finding Things Out. He took a small torch from the pocket of his gown and closed the door of the shed behind him, so that its dim light could not be seen from the house. He cast the beam around him, checking that he was alone, knowing that he was alone, but checking all the same. He knew what he was looking for, and where to find it — under the workbench. The canister sloshed, about half-full. He set the torch down on the bench to illuminate his work, and poured a little of the canister's contents onto his hands. It was viscous, slimy, not at all as he had expected. He rubbed it onto his dressing gown, and set to work. The plant pots wouldn't do because they had holes in them, so he found an empty paint tin and filled the bottom with petrol.

The matches were in his other dressing gown pocket, stolen from the kitchen cupboard that his Mother forgot he was tall enough to reach. His hands did not even shake as he struck one and dropped it into the tin. The effect was instant, glorious. The flames shot up and then faded back, dancing like the ballerina in a music box. He stood, mesmerised, barely even noticing when his dressing gown caught. It must have been one second, two seconds, three seconds before he felt the heat on his thigh, then he started screaming.

He ripped off the gown and threw it to the floor, nearly knocking the tin over. He huddled down, shocked, and watched as tin and gown consumed themselves, throwing distorted shadows on the walls. Mother arrived minutes later, shrieking at the top of her voice, but he was in no danger. The burn on his thigh would transmute itself into a silver scar, marking where the fire kissed him.

David was sitting at his desk. A spreadsheet was giving him trouble; the numbers of crates of printer toner that should be bound for Birmingham refused to match up with the numbers that were recorded leaving the warehouse. The fact that this mattered so much was depressing. Dinklage, the boss-man, blustered up to David's desk and made savage gestures at him with sheets of paper. His face turned red the way it would if someone were to hold a candle underneath his hostile, blubbery chin. The problem may not have been Birmingham. David's gaze kept slipping to the waste bin, which seemed to make Dinklage think that he was ignoring him. It was so difficult to care.

When Dinklage gave up and walked away, threats of discipline still hot on his lips, David returned to the spreadsheet. Another ten minutes and the numbers were still refusing to resolve themselves. The waste bin became more inviting, but he couldn't do it there. He got up from his swivel chair and made for the break room. He walked over to the pile of newspapers and glossy magazines on the corner of the table and took out his lighter. It was silver and monogramed; it cost £55. It would light even in gale-force wind.

Looking around to check that there was no-one else in the room, David held the lighter to the stack.

The cheap toner used in daily newspapers meant that the stack caught quickly. He took a cigarette from his pocket, ripped it in half, and tossed the bottom half into the conflagration as a Probable Cause — someone having a surreptitious smoke without going out in the rain. He stood back, watching for as long as he dared. The flames were tipped with dark grey smoke, standing six inches proud of their fuel. A few charred shreds floated upwards like ascending angels. He took a damp tea towel from beside the sink and threw it over the pile. He just had time to slip out of the back door and join the milling crowds outside before the smoke alarms went off.

Week 4 — Dialogue

Dialogue is difficult. Dialogue is not your friend.

'David. David, are you listening to me?' A drop of spittle flew from Dinklage's mouth and flecked the page he waved.

'Yes sir.' The standard answer.

'Then why are you doing nothing about it, man?'

'I shall get right on to it, sir.'

'You just see that you do — Polytech has our nuts in a vice. They're edging us out of the market.'

He could have said anything. David was tuning out. He turned to his spreadsheet and keyed in numbers. Dinklage had no idea if they were correct. David knew they were not.

'You've been letting it slide, David. Pull yourself together or it'll be you for the chopper.'

'Immediately, sir.' Autopilot was fully engaged.

Week 5 — Setting

The head office of StapleMate Office Supplies Ltd was like a set of Chinese boxes — cubicles in cubes.

Each of the cubicles had a desk with a dated computer beside a filing cabinet for storing pointless pieces of paper about other pieces of paper and staples and paperclips. The drone of the ceiling fans and the whir of computers were constant and turned the air into a nerve-jangling hum that pushed on the brain like a tumour. The air smelled of Heinz tomato soup, burnt coffee and toner.

David's house was OK, which was part of the problem. He had spent seven years of his life working and saving up to buy it, and it was nobody's but his own. It was one of a row of identical semi-detached houses. The ground floor was open-plan; an adjustable leather armchair sat a perfect distance from an HD television and a high-range sound system. The cookware in the kitchen went virtually untouched. On the glass dining table stood an elegant cruet, flanking an empty vase. A study in chrome and white.

   The house represented the culmination of his life thus far, and he hated it. His bookshelves were stacked with unread classics in attractive covers. His CD collection failed utterly to define him as a person. All of his things were carefully arranged to make it appear as though he had a life, when in fact all he had was *stuff*. He needed to work, and he had to work for something, so he bought *stuff*.

Week 6 — Dialogue

Dialogue is invented speech. People do not talk in books as they do in real life; it would be too annoying to read and would not make sense.
   'How often do you think of fire, David?' she asked. Clipped consonants.
   'Less, now.'

'You know that these thoughts are unhealthy, yes.' Not a question. He gave no answer. He stared, she tapped. Tap, tap, tap.

'I would like you to try something for me,' she said. Speech tags help the reader to follow the flow of the conversation. 'When you think of setting a fire, I would like you to vocalise the word 'no'. It is the first step in recognising the thoughts as negative.'

'You're the therapist.'

'Very good. Pyromania is simply an impulse control disorder. I believe that with the correct combination of CBT and selective serotonin reuptake inhibitors, these impulses can be managed.'

'I'm sure you're right. Being here, with all this quiet, I am feeling calmer already,' he lied.

'Quite. Also, have you heard that we will be visited soon by a man by the name of Joshua Finch? He will be running a writing course with some of the patients; it could be very helpful for you, to find a more healthy method of expressing your feelings.'

'I may have seen a notice somewhere.'

'Do you think that will be a problem for you, David?'

'No.' Her head was anointed with a tongue of fire.

Week 7 — Character

Dr. Maloney, M. (Mary) had a brass plaque on her desk that lists off the letters after her name (14, in groups of 2 or 3). An accoutrement of an ego that was masturbatory in its self-indulgence. She found time in her schedule to keep her nails manicured and painted red, a gloss red like cherries. Her lips too, red. Her ginger hair bunched severely on top of her head. The odd wisp of it escapes the bun

and floats upwards. It looks as though it is on fire.
I picture her head on fire. She looks at me over
the top of rimless Swiss glasses and smiles as her
skin blisters. She is doing this only to excite me.

David is older now, nearly 28. He spends most of his
time being bored and dissatisfied with the way his
life has turned out. He gets terribly anxious about his
interactions with other people; sometimes his words
come out of his mouth before he has had a chance
to consider them properly. The people probably talk
about him behind his back. His colleagues play
tricks on him at work, which could be camaraderie,
but they laugh *at him* rather than *with him*.

    Thoughts in his head — cars pull into petrol
stations all the time. People put the pumps into their
cars. They watch the numbers on the screens cycle
higher and higher. Few of them could even tell you
what colour petrol is. As far as they are concerned it
could be an imaginary substance that everybody
just assumes is real. We only know about it because
of its effects. The car leaves the station. Smog rises.
Every so often, something catches fire.

Week 8 — Action

David stared at the ceiling. He was lying on a leather
couch in Dr. Maloney's office, trying hard not to look
into her smug face. She tapped a pencil against
her clipboard during the lull in conversation, slightly
out of time with the second-hand ticking of the
clock. The effect was syncopated, maddening. They
talked for half an hour, every other day, despite
the fact that there was nothing to do in Bloomfield,
and so there was nothing he could have done since
they last spoke. He thought about running, but
there were guards to stop that kind of thing — huge

men in nurse's scrubs. He was trapped with the clicking pencil and the ticking clock and Maloney's smug face.

He had fantasised about it for months, planning it meticulously: taking the sheaves of pointless hardbacks from their shelves and scattering them across the floor in savage circles, toppling the CD racks in an act of iconoclasm. He emptied a gallon of petrol across the floor, across the leather armchair, the kitchen. The words 'dinosaur soup' played on repeat in his head. Before he left, he turned on the gas rings of the hob without pressing the ignition. He took out his lighter; it would be his beloved sacrifice. Outside the door, he clicked it; the spark was instantaneous, as always. He tossed it inside, closed the door, and waited.

When the fire crews arrived, the blaze had climbed out of the upper floor windows and onto the roof. They found David sitting cross-legged in the street, watching his life go up in flames. He was smiling. The fire had spoken to him like the burning bush, promising him great things, if only he would trust it. If only he would let it into his heart.

The firemen were speaking to him. One of them had pressed an oxygen mask into his hand and was trying to get him to inhale. They were asking him questions — was he alright, did he know what had happened. Someone in the background was screaming, or maybe it was a siren. Policemen arrived, hoisting him from the ground. David could see firemen dousing his work with jets of water. He resented them; this was his moment. They were walking with profane feet on his hallowed ground.

Alex Marsh

Fidelity

I am almost sure that it was my idea to come here. A grey sky looms behind the distorted glass of the cottage window, and if I stand on my toes I can just about see the crags below jutting their chins into the sea. A bird's dark body flickers in and out of existence in the rippled glass. A large seagull, perhaps, gorged on the slippery silver hauls of the tired fishing boats along the coast.

The kitchen is an utter mess. A measuring jug still lies on its side where Leanne knocked it over in a rush to save the pancakes I was burning. The batter has spilled onto the table, and has now dried and congealed; the surface has cracked to reveal a glistening wetness underneath. As she struggled into her coat, Leanne had hissed that there might as well be batter on the ceiling, for all the good I was at making breakfast. We should have just bought something at the village shop.

I fetch the mop and sweep it over the sticky floor. I want the evidence of my uselessness to be gone before she gets back. Whilst looking down it's quite easy to ignore the charred mess slopped over the Aga, and the gleaming china plates still waiting on the kitchen table.

One evening, Leanne had exploded into our flat clutching a letter, and announced that she had a job offer from Florida.

The groan of London traffic drifted through our front door — which she had left open — and dulled my shock. She seemed to expect me to be ecstatic about this, so I gave her a tight hug and murmured congratulations in her ear. But when I put the kettle on, my thoughts seethed and spat along with its boiling water. She must have forgotten, then, that we couldn't move to America. We wouldn't get a spouse's Green Card.

By the time I added the milk, our tea was cold, with a sheen like oil clouding over the surface. In the bated silence of the flat — Leanne must have finally shut the door — it occurred to me that she might not be thinking of taking me along at all. Maybe she was thinking long-distance, or a bitch of a commute, or something.

From then on the letter planted itself at the top of our dining table like a stuck-up, uninvited guest. Often I caught Leanne twitching it this way and that to keep the thick, water-marked sheet perfectly aligned. Whenever I came home and saw it, or ate my lunch alone, I wondered whether Leanne's lab partners had already moved out to America, with Visas, and clip-lock boxes full of all their sentimental crap. At some point I stopped turning on Radio Four to keep me company while I ate, and took to staring at the letter instead, daring myself to actually read it.

When Leanne was home to have dinner with me, I found myself sweaty and flustered, with my stomach too knotted to eat anything. Perhaps this is how I would have behaved, had Leanne's parents been alive to look down their nose at me, to scrutinise and ignore me by turns; to ask me whether I had settled into London yet, to tell me that the lifestyle wasn't for everyone.

When I accidentally knocked my orange juice over one morning, the stain crept across the letter like a siege upon a frontier. Leanne had yelled at me and snatched the letter away as I tried to blot at it with kitchen paper. I muttered an apology but couldn't stop staring. It felt like I'd broken some kind of stalemate.

'Are you going to move to Florida?' I blurted as Leanne dabbed at the letter.

She shrugged. Maybe. The ceiling seemed to be pressing me hard into my chair.

'Let's go away together,' I said.

'What?' Leanne asked, exasperated.

'Somewhere we haven't been before,' I invented desperately. 'Rent a cottage for a weekend. We could go on long walks, and get some space, some fresh air.'

Leanne laughed despite herself. 'Like in nursery? Playing at being Wife and Wife?'

I shrugged, trying to seem calm.

'Yeh, why not.'

'Fine, whatever,' said Leanne, turning back to the letter. She gingerly picked it up and clipped it to the notice board to dry before disappearing to the bathroom.

A tiny bloom of adrenalin had pulsed through me as I thought of a cottage in Cornwall, surrounded by the vast blue of oceans and wheeling birds. We could wake up each morning like we used to, before Leanne got her early morning start at the lab, with her reaching for me before she was even half awake, folding me back into the sleepy warmth of the duvet.

I'm trying to shove the cupboard door shut on the flailing mop when Leanne starts rattling her keys in the door. She brings a gust of sea-salted drizzle and a white plastic bag into the cottage with her. I help unknot her various hoods from her scarf whilst she grumbles about the bloody Cornish summer. Without her coat Leanne hunches her shoulders over, as if it's chilly in the cottage. She skates a glance over the floor, and when she doesn't find any pancake mess, she mutters a thanks and turns away. I just shrug, but I don't think she sees.

'Pain-au-chocolat,' says Leanne, spilling brown paper bags onto the table. They are covered in grease blots. We sit opposite each other, which feels odd and formal, but the pastries are butterslick and sweet. Leanne is industriously retrieving each scattered flake by licking the tip of her finger and sticking the food to the glistening saliva. I can see smears of spit and fat on the table, illuminated in the glare of the overhead lights.

'Shall we go for a walk in the village today?' I suggest when Leanne is finished licking. We finished driving so late last night that I haven't been outside yet.

'Sure,' says Leanne. 'It's still traditional, not all touristy. You'll like it.'

'You did just go to the village though,' I point out.

'Do you mind?'

'I can get us there, then.' says Leanne as she screws our rubbish into a ball and stuffs it in the bin.

She is the first to escape the confines of the cottage and venture back out into the spitting rain. My fingers scrabble at the wall next to the door, automatically seeking the alarm box of our London flat. I snatch my hand from the wall, but Leanne is staring through next-door's windows and doesn't notice. Annoyed and guilty, I yank the key from my bag and slam the door. Right now I don't want anything to remind Leanne of London, or the letter, or going back home. I can feel that my face is flushed — the wind has an extra bite when it hits my skin — but if Leanne notices she doesn't say anything.

It's not too far to the village. I stretch to take Leanne's hand before realising that she's shoved them deep in her pockets. On impulse I do the same, and hope that she doesn't think my jerky movements are defensive. I joke that Leanne should have packed the gloves I gave her last Christmas.

'What?' she snaps back.

The walk is claustrophobic, and I try to come up with ludicrous reasons as to why the Cornish build such high and close walls in which to trap their roads. It's for the smuggling trade, so that laden carts could move unseen. It's because there weren't any other jobs going, after the tin mines collapsed. It's because once, the winds were so strong that a child was blown clean off a cliff, and their body was never found.

'Could you even imagine swimming in that sea?' asks Leanne. I peer through the hedge, where she's looking. There are sprays of colour dotted on top of the waves.

'Surfers. They're bloody mad,' she says. The waves are rearing back, bunching up, getting ready to crash back down onto the beach.

'You like swimming, Leanne,' I say, irritated by her bad mood. 'It's a beautiful view, though.'

'Not beautiful,' Leanne disagrees, 'brutal. How many people do you think die every year off the coast?' The chequered flags of the lifeguards do seem dwarfed by the broiling waves.

'But this view is just ours,' I say. 'No one else has ever seen the ocean quite like this.'

Leanne tilts her head, considering. 'Still brutal, though. And deadly,' she adds. 'Just because it's far away, doesn't make it pretty.'

I wonder if she will miss me when she goes to Florida, and for one wild moment I think I am going to cry, right here in the middle of the lane. But Leanne's bored now, and she marches off without me. It's raining a little harder, so I don't entirely blame her. Anyway, my toes are numb from the water seeping through my trainers.

We stumble into the village shop in a flurry of wet coats. The ceiling is low, throwing gloom into every corner, and a mint-green, speckled lino doesn't quite disguise the grime at the feet of the aisles. Our footprints leave a dirty trail as we meander around the shop.

'What did we come in here for anyway?' she asks, without actually looking at me.

'A rustic and traditional Cornwall,' I mutter.

Leanne scowls and grabs a couple of bargain Pringle tubes from the shelf before stalking to the till. When she hands over a twenty, the shop lady is obviously disgruntled. She pinches it with disgust and spends a long time examining the watermarks. Eventually Leanne coughs and the lady bangs the cash register open. She counts change into Leanne's waiting hand with a pointed lack of speed, until there is a small mountain of coins that's threatening to avalanche.

'Old bag,' Leanne says as she turns away. The lady steps back a little, as if she has been slapped. I hurry forwards and move Leanne out of the way, my hands on her waist. The lady narrows her eyes.

'May I have some stamps, please?' I ask, laying it on thick. She shrugs but totters away to the post office till. Her dishwater-green bib reminds me of the dinner-ladies at school, and I feel guilty, like I am trying to scam an extra dessert.

'What do you want stamps for?' Leanne asks. She is closer to me than I thought and I start a little, stubbing my toe into the counter.

'I thought I'd write to my parents,' I say, reaching to squeeze Leanne's hand. 'You know, to let them know what it's like in sunny Cornwall.'

'What, an intel report?' Leanne flinches away from my hand and glares at me. 'You never talk to them. So are you just going to lie outright, or did you think that you would go for the most depressing postcard ever?'

I think of the pancake disaster, and the near-silent drive down from London. All I can see are the coloured speckles on the floor. Perhaps I can find a repeating pattern.

'They're probably hoping this trip will end it,' Leanne mutters.

'Family holiday, is it?' interrupts a quivering, snooty voice. I turn to stare at the dinner lady. She is flicking her clouding eyes between me and Leanne, looking for a resemblance.

'Oh no, we're not sisters,' I say firmly before Leanne can speak. 'Just friends. Thought we'd get away from the London chaos for a while. You know, come and see your *beautiful* beaches and blue skies.'

'Excuse me?' Leanne hisses behind me. I ignore her. The dinner lady nods and hands me some stamps.

'That's four pounds ninety, please.'

I grab for my purse as Leanne stalks past me and

wrenches open the shop door. After throwing a fiver onto the counter, I rush out after her, not waiting for the change. It's only when the shop is swallowed by the slimed mist that I realise I have forgotten to buy a postcard.

I follow Leanne to the nearest pub — it's either that or the church. Inside it's empty and dim. Leanne ignores me when I suggest a table near the bar, and heads back outside. Each pub is the same as the first — it seems that's all there is in this stupid village — and each time I suggest we sit and talk, Leanne is off again, storming through the village with me traipsing after her.

Eventually she stops. A figure in an old Macintosh is hunched in the doorway of the town hall like a gargoyle. They gesture for us to come inside and Leanne disappears through the door. The town hall is mostly empty, and the lingering dust of stagnant decades makes me cough. Huddled in the corner is a drab display of coastal-themed photographs; bright little price tags stuck optimistically on the frames.

'Look Martha,' Leanne says, pointing to a photo-graph.'Isn't this one just lovely? It's so realistic and vivid. Just lovely.'

I cross the empty hall, footsteps echoing. It's a picture of three fish. One lies beheaded, its body blunted except for a protruding fragment of translucent spine. Another had had its belly slit open, and its intestines are slumped against the edge of the frame, reeking.

'God Leanne, now I feel sick.' My eyes are hooked on the spilled bowels.

'So do I Martha,' says Leanne, her voice hard. 'Look, I'm sorry, but I didn't see you standing up to her.'

'It was an honest question. There was nothing to stand up to!'

Leanne is leaning in front of me, the table swaying, her hair falling onto photographs of dead fish. I want to yell at her. What was I supposed to say? Our life is none of her business! But Leanne gets there first, and asks a different question.

'Are you embarrassed because of us?'

My glare wilts. I don't have to say it. She backs away and heads for the door.

'It'll be even worse if you move to Florida,' I say.

'Maybe,' Leanne concedes, pulling the hood of her coat back up. 'But then, maybe there won't be a problem at all.'

She walks out of the town hall. This time I don't follow — I feel like if I catch up with her she might spin and smack me. Instead, I crawl around the village in the rain, trying to find some pub in which to hide until the dampness of my clothes seizes my joints in place.

When I step through the front door, Leanne is waiting at the kitchen table. Her presence makes the rooms seem smaller, like the high Cornish walls are still bearing down upon me. I try to take off my drenched coat with as few movements as possible, as we skirt around each other. She's heated some soup in the pan for us, but it has turned to a sludge with a skin shrinking from the edges of the pan. She must have been waiting a while for me to come back.

'I was getting worried,' she whispers, not moving from her chair. I mutter an apology for ruining the soup. She says that it's fine, and that she isn't that hungry anyway. We look at each other for a moment, tasting each other's mood like a snake flicking its tongue.

I head straight to bed, and curl up under the covers still fully dressed. When I wake in the middle of the night, there is still a vast and empty space beside me.

In the morning, the sun dredges a blue sky up from the depths of the ocean. I stay in bed for a while, exhaustion and the clinging damp of my clothes making me feel sick. As long as I don't roll over I can pretend like everything is normal. I can't remember the last time we didn't sleep together. I feel twitchy but calm, as if I know that a tsunami is about to hit and am observing the seething, rolling mass from the fragile shoreline.

When I do eventually creep downstairs, I find Leanne asleep on the arm of the sofa, her head pillowed on a book. I wrap a rug around my shoulders and ghost through the kitchen making some coffee. Slick as anything, I accidentally drop the coffee jar on the work surface with a heart-stopping smash — exploding glass and coffee granules everywhere.

'Shit, Martha!' Leanne has started awake and is rubbing her cheek. I stare at the mess, unable to believe I can screw even this up. The kettle clicks off. Its roar of boiling water subsides. Leanne just looks at me, then coughs up a small laugh and smiles. Relieved, I fetch the dust pan and brush from the cupboard again. I've cleaned this place more than I do our flat.

We sit at the table, sipping coffee and staring out of the window. I've a crick in my neck from having to turn to see it, but I don't think I can look at Leanne, so I rest my chin in my palm and wait it out.

'Maybe we can go swimming today,' Leanne suggests.

'It won't be too cold for you?'

'Maybe,' says Leanne. I remember her swearing at the surfers yesterday. 'But I've got to at least try it.'

I shrug and push my mug onto the side.

'I'll go and get changed then,' I say as I head towards the stairs.

Leanne shouts that the wetsuits are in the red case. This irritates me. I know this. I was the one who bought and packed them when I realised my old suit would definitely not fit either of us.

When we're both ready we slip through the gate at the bottom of the cottage's miniature garden and wade through a field of tangled grass to get to the coastal path. We ignore the rusting and crooked sign that specifies a recommended safe distance from the cliff edge. I've never once had an accident. Even my parents used to think they were overcautious.

It is only a short scramble down the sharp rocks, until we are pressed against a damp and seeping wall with the roiling ocean at our feet. With each wave the water floods onto our rocky platform. Icy tendrils are creeping up my wetsuit legs from my drenched neoprene boots. We watch the water battering the smoothed rocks. Neither one of us seems to want to go in first.

I squint at the murky horizon. There are no birds in the sky today.

'It feels like there is no one else in the world,' says Leanne, sounding awed. 'And it doesn't look so bad, when it's not raining.' A particularly vicious wave breaks over our shins.

'We're going back to London tomorrow morning,' I remind her. Leanne narrows her eyes at me.

'Yeh,' she says, and takes a running leap at the broiling water. As soon as she goes under, it feels as though the tension has snapped. I enjoy breathing the brisk, salt-laden air into my lungs until Leanne surfaces again, her arms and legs frenzied and thrashing against the waves.

'No one here to see us drown,' yells Leanne over the sea's roar. 'I'm completely trusting you to save me.'

She's grinning, and trying to keep her bobbing head out of the water. When it floods her mouth, she spits and paddles her frenetic limbs harder like a ridiculous, spasming puppet on top of the water. She is panting, and snot has dribbled out of her nose as the salt water streams from her. For a moment she is pounded down by an incoming wave, and I can see her dark outline spiral in the ceaseless rolling grip of the water. She comes up spluttering. I don't move to help her, but imagine instead that this fragment of ocean already writhing between us is the entire Atlantic.

I am not worried. She is a strong swimmer, and looking down on her affords me a savage pleasure more exhilarating than a brutal sea. When Leanne realises that I am not going to jump in as well, she catches a wave and sails onto the rocks with ease. She shivers all of the way back; we forgot to bring towels. I wonder if she will ask why I didn't want to swim. When she doesn't, though, I am not surprised.

Leanne is in the shower when I pick up the book she was using as a pillow last night. A piece of folded paper pokes out the ends — a makeshift bookmark — and I know it's going to be her letter, even before I open it.

Congratulations, you have been successful in your application to Meryl-Jones Laboratories.

Not a job offer, then. She applied. I pace around the kitchen, furious. The thought that she doesn't want me keeps lurching up my swollen throat like a tide. I want the hurl the letter into the ocean — get rid of it. So I do the next best thing, and throw it in the sink.

The paper collapses in soft, sodden folds under the gush of the faucet. It becomes blushed with water stains. The ink begins to run. I take the scrubbing brush and swipe it gently over the paper's surface. As the wet fibres roll into little bobbles, its words mush together and disappear. I leave the logo at the top of the page. I want her to find it, and know it was me. That, in the end, it was my choice.

Leanne finds me shivering on the beach. I am bundled into a woolly hat and jumpers, but my jeans are soaked from paddling. I shrink away from her, but she stops just out of arm's reach and gazes at me.

'That was pathetic, Martha.' Her voice is soft, caught up on the wind. She is calm as she explains that she already answered the letter. That she'll be gone within the month.

She begins to walk away, following the shoreline, but turns after a few steps.

'I'll get the train back to London. You can take the car.'

I stare after her until she is merely a dark body picking its way over rocks, toothpick arms waving for balance. Her footsteps are like a seam, stitching the sand to the waves. Even standing under this hollow sky, I can't seem to imagine enough space between us.

Catriona McLean

Lungs

Whitby awoke to a corpse on the beach. A crowd had gathered around her already, wrapped tight in raincoats and wellingtons, staring at the body slumped on the slate-grey sand. It must have been the storm that killed her. That summer had been the worst in decades; worse than when Irene was a little girl, and the waves had surged all the way up to the quay and left slashes of brown across the bright cottage fronts.

Irene watched the town unfurl from her kitchen window. Children in bright red macs clung to parents' hands, pointing at the body. It was a pitiful sight. Her grey mass lay stripped of all dignity, naked and shapeless in the drizzle, and her head had been caved in. Irene's throat tightened with pity when a lorry pulled up to the shore and men in fluorescent jackets clambered out of it, barking at the gawping tourists to stand back.

She must have been young, Irene thought — six metres at most. After a lifetime spent on the coast, Irene could tell any species by sight. This was a fin whale: she belonged in the open sea, where she was weightless, where the pressing sand could never crush the air from her lungs. Irene turned from the window to clear away her breakfast crockery and put on her coat. Before she left the cottage, she checked the mirror to make sure her hat fully hid her thinning scrub of hair. From the pathway that led down to the town, Irene had a clear view of the men still struggling to haul the carcass away, until the faint rain prickled against her eyes and she was forced to look away.

Irene found herself in her usual haunt, nestled by the window, the local paper laid across the stained white table. Families squalled around her and the reek of chip fat and vinegar made Irene want to gasp for fresh air, but she clung to her mug of tea and waited for her daughter to arrive, as promised, from York. The paper talked of renovations to the Church of Saint Mary, and of the recent appeal to prevent peddlers from overrunning the beach — as if that would somehow make the town peaceful again. On the fourth page, she was met again by the sight of the sprawling carcass, now in grisly definition. WHALE BEACHINGS LINKED TO CLIMATE CHANGE, the headline warned. Poor thing must have been there overnight, if the papers had already got to her. Irene thought of the journalists taking their photographs and leaving her alone and helpless for the world to deal with the next day.

Helen arrived late, flustered, wearing a navy suit.

'I thought you had the morning off,' Irene said.

'I did.' Helen sat opposite her and waved her hand for the waitress to refill the teapot. 'I had to pop into the office to sort out the pitch for Monday. Mark was supposed to oversee that, but we all know how reliable he is.'

Mark was Helen's husband. Together they ran a travel agent's back in York, which specialised in renting twee seaside cottages to fresh-faced families who longed to 'get back to basics.' Her fit of rebellion against her mother's own dislike for tourists had worked surprisingly well for her — Helen was far better off than Irene had ever been; but she was Frank's daughter too. She had his determination.

Irene attempted a motherly smile. 'Well, perhaps you should have a word with him.'

'Already have.' Helen sipped hastily at her tea. 'You look tired, Mum. Have you been taking your medication?'

'Which medication?' Her throat took a daily battering from a cocktail of tablets. Frank had often quipped she may as well go down to the beach and swallow pebbles there for all the good it did her. Irene watched the rainwater dribble down the window, her thoughts drawing back to the stranded whale, gasping for breath as she crushed herself into the earth — the panic — mud filling her mouth, as if she were being buried alive. How long would it take to die?

'Are you listening to me?' Helen was saying. She reached over for the paper, glancing over the article. 'Shame. That'll put people off coming here.'

'Encourage them, more like,' said Irene. 'You should have seen them all gathered around, gawking. I even heard someone telling their child it might explode.'

She winced. Helen began to explain that it actually happened sometimes, but by then Irene was thinking of what Frank would make of the whole situation. He'd been a fisherman when he was young, back when fishing in the North Sea was worth its while.

'You remember the story your father told about his fishing days, don't you?' Irene said.

Helen shrugged, exactly as she would have done when she was sixteen. 'I remember it was more exaggerated every time he told it, just like all his stories. Have I told you about all the drama with planning permission in Scarborough?'

Irene listened to her daughter, nodding along, until their tea was finished and they left to walk back along the promenade. The rolling hum of waves drumming in from the beach drowned out the sound of Helen's worries, but the walk grew more difficult every time Irene did it, even though the ground was level. When they reached the hill, Irene's heart was burning in her chest. She leaned against the railings to catch her breath.

'We ought to talk about the house.'

Helen's eyes flicked over the rising cliff side, where the white cottage sat, pebble-flecked and grown with ivy, overlooking the sweeping waves below.

An accusing look entered her eyes.

'What do you mean?'

'I've been talking to a man about selling it.'

Whenever Helen went quiet it meant she was angry. She'd been that way since she was a child, taking a furious vow of silence if she was denied her own way. Irene and Frank had savage fights over it in the past. 'You coddle her,' she used to tell him, and he'd just laugh and call her a harridan.

'Selling it,' Helen repeated.

'There's been a few nice couples who're thinking of retiring here,' Irene said.

'You still live here! Where on earth do you think you'd go?'

'Not to yours, if that's what you're worried about. Let's be serious now. Soon enough, I'll be gone, and I need to think about what will happen afterwards. The money will go to you, of course.'

'Don't be so morbid.' She rolled her eyes. 'You're only seventy-six. I can't believe you sometimes. The house would be a great asset!'

'To your business, yes, I'm sure it would. I've seen all those lovely young women with their lovely young husbands walking past and admiring the *authenticity*.' She could see it now. They'd laugh about how quaint it all was, quarrel over the morality of feeding their children chip butties ('It supports the local community!' 'But they're *fried*!') And then they'd scoot back off to their suburbs and leave her home dead and empty.

'And what about me?' Helen was saying. 'You just assume I'll put it in the business. This is *my* childhood. What if I want to come back to it?'

'For good? While you still have children to raise? I don't think so.'

'In the summer—'

'Yes, and what about the rest of the year? Empty. I can't bear it. My home, empty, with nothing but rain for company.' Empty. The word echoed. 'I won't have it. This is a home that needs *life*.'

Helen started digging in her handbag for her keys. 'Life,' she sneered. 'I'm your family. I'm the life that should be here, who deserves to be here after all I've done for you.' By then she was already stalking towards the car, heels clipping against the cobblestones. Before she got in, she turned back. 'Dad would *never* do this. You know that?'

He would have, Irene thought but did not say. He would never let people flit in and out of *their* home like they had never been there.

Helen didn't call for a full two weeks. Irene supposed, when she sat in front of the television screen pretending not to count the hours since she'd heard a real voice, that she could break the silence — but that wasn't her way. That would mean she'd lost.

She was a young girl again, falling from a great height into an immeasurably vast expanse, plummeting so quickly that the wind whipped the scream straight from her throat. When she hit the surface it shattered like a mirror and she plunged below, into freezing water. She floundered, her lungs clenching in shock. Her mouth and nose filled with brine. She lunged for the surface but it was already pulling away from her, as she was hauled further and further below by the weight of her clothes. Every mad toss of her body took the air further away from her.

The water was icy clear and ringing with an echo like creaking hulls. Irene saw it, far away, so distant but so enormous — impossibly huge, larger than anything that could ever live and breathe, so large that she knew she must be dreaming. The shape passed below her, a sleek black mass of serpentine grace. It moved slowly, forcefully, its fluke rising and falling in rhythm with the waves. Panic trickled into Irene's lungs. She felt the pressure of water crushing her ribcage as she descended and the glittered surface faded into twilight. The shape passed overhead, rumbling, moaning — the sound crackles through the water, hammering through Irene's skull —

— She opened her mouth, felt her heart bursting for breath, her brain pounding and screaming, felt her ribs buckling inside her —

Irene awoke, breathing hard and clutching her chest. Lamp on. Glass of water on side. She took a sip and waited for the pain to subside, but her heart was thrumming and her breath escaped her in ragged, uneven whistles. Her phone was on the bedside table, where Helen had once told her to put it. *Just in case you need me.*

'Hello?' Helen's voice said, after two rings. 'Hello?' She sounded afraid.

Irene opened her mouth but only a choking sound came out.

'Mum — is that you? Mum? What's wrong? Do you want me to call an ambulance?'

Irene's fear switched in an instant. Her throat was still tight but it all had just been panic. Everything was going back to normal. She could feel her heart slowing, her head clearing. 'It's me,' she said. 'I'm sorry, I was a little confused, I didn't mean to —'

'You're not breathing properly. I'm going to call an ambulance.'

Irene looked helplessly at the receiver. 'Don't! I'm fine. It was an accident.'

'Calling me at three in the morning is not an accident. You can't breathe properly: you are not fine.'

'I don't need an ambulance!'

'Wait there. I'll come over myself.'

Helen arrived in tracksuit bottoms, looking strangely vulnerable now that she was bereft of her suit and heels. She fretted over Irene's breathing, clucking and flinging her hands to and fro, which only made the whole thing worse. Helen insisted they go to the hospital. She threw some of Irene's spare underwear and a toothbrush into a bag — just in case — then led Irene over to the car, still fussing as she helped her into the front seat.

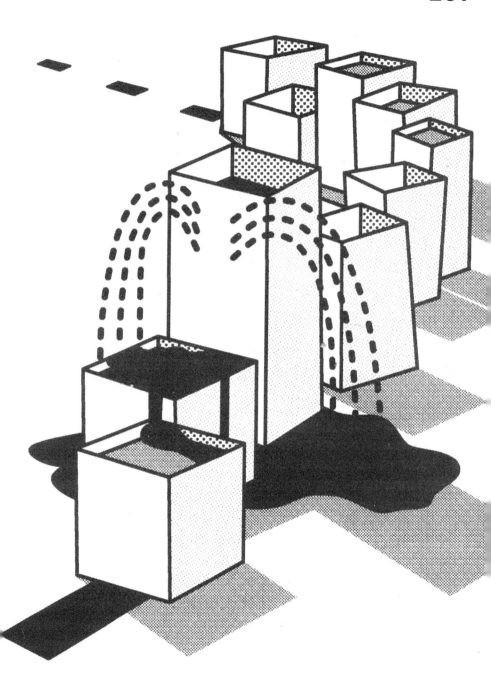

'I've been staying at the White Horse,' Helen admitted. 'I've had a lot of work on here; I didn't want to put upon you — and — well. You know. You're lucky I was around.'

Irene said nothing. It had been years since Irene saw the town at this hour. The last time had been with Frank, close to her ruby wedding, when the whole town suffered from a power-cut and they'd wrapped up warm and climbed to the church, to see the stars and sea as if towns didn't exist. Now everything was still and silent, muffled by the clouds overhead, and even the streetlamps seemed distant. The local hospital was unavailable this late at night: York was the closest emergency service. Helen drove stoically on, her face tight with determination — but Irene, filled with guilt at how well she was feeling, could only think of her bed.

She'd be wasting their time. There was nothing wrong with her above being a decrepit old bag, and they'd tell her so if they knew she'd made her daughter drive her all the way to York for feeling a little puffed out. 'We should turn back,' Irene said. 'This isn't an emergency.'

'For God's sake. Stop being so proud and accept that you need to see a doctor.'

'They'll tell you I'm fine and this will all be for nothing. You should go home and get some sleep.'

'I'm not getting out of bed at three in the morning because you've called me in a state, and then turn back halfway to the bloody hospital!'

They were nowhere near halfway. They weren't even at the dual carriageway yet. 'You'll be wasting more time if you get there just to be turned away.'

Helen's eyes flicked to the side. She slowed, turning into the nearest corner, then pulled up as soon as she was able. She stared at the wheel, her mouth tight with suppressed anger. Then she looked Irene up and down, scrutinising her. 'You really are fine, aren't you?'

'I was just a little panicked. I was dreaming —'

'You dragged me out of bed at this hour for a bloody false alarm. I can't believe you. I literally can *not* believe you.'

Irene dared to mention that it was not her idea to go to the hospital, and that she'd just wanted to hear her daughter's voice; Helen asked how she was supposed to have interpreted it, and on it went, the pair of them snapping away at one another right until Helen dropped Irene off back at her gate. She stopped long enough to help her mother out of the front seat, then, still growling about how she needed to be up at seven, got back into the car and screeched away. Irene waited up in the kitchen, pressing a glass of water close to her mouth until the sound of wheels faded, and the stillness grew, and all she could hear was the distant hiss of the sea.

Her lungs were failing, a gruelling process, slow and inevitable, like being buried alive. She'd known it for months. Or years, why not? What was the point of dragging it out? No need to be a coward. Frank hadn't been. When Death came for him, he'd met him head on.

It had gone something like this:

Death came scything into the room, his claws outstretched for Frank, who sat reading his paper. Frank looked up, a grizzled eyebrow arching. 'Now there's a mug that could do with a drink,' he said. He folded his paper, slowly, deliberately, while Death watched. Then he stood and reached for the decanter on the mantelpiece. 'This'll put the spark back in your eyes. Glenfarclas. Fifteen years. Been saving it for this very day.'

Death lowered his scythe and took the whiskey. He downed it in one, grimacing. The ruddy fluid trickled out from between his rusted ribcage.

'Takes like Satan's bathtub,' said Death.

They laughed. Frank invited Death to a game of poker, in exchange for a year or two. Death sat. He still clutched his scythe. They played for hours, Frank's nerve unwavering. 'All in,' he said, clutching his double Kings.

Death's empty sockets glared over the ace and queen held between his claws. 'Met.'

Frank saw the cold black fire burning between those hollow eyes and moved aside, roaring, as Death leaped up and swiped for Frank with his scythe. Bellowing, Frank got Death in a headlock, pummelling the base of his skull — the skeleton twisted, hissing, the scythe skittering out of his reach. Frank carried on punching but Death broke free, seized the scythe, and swung it in a deadly arch that breaks right through Frank's ribs. Frank fell back, straight onto his armchair, clutching his chest and knocking over his beautiful decanter. Death, swearing and dizzy, legged it out the open window. Irene entered moments later, saw Frank motionless on the armchair, the shock of betrayal still on his face, and screamed.

It was a ridiculous fabrication, she realised, like a Norman Wisdom sketch. She told it to herself that way because she couldn't imagine the reality. Frank was too bold and full of life to die drunk and alone in his chair. It was the only way to cope, to meet Death head on and laugh in his face.

When the day came, she knew she was ready. She could see the 'Sold' sign swaying outside, where the last fading rays shone through the clouds and caught on the sign's patent sheen. Helen had accepted it, eventually. There were plenty of cottages like it, she'd ended up saying; she could come back to Whitby at any time. It was a lie. There was nowhere like their home. Helen had cried when Irene told her.

The curtains closed. She tried to imagine new voices in her kitchen, or new bodies in her bed, or new coats bustling together beneath the stairs, but her mind wouldn't stay on them. Lying in bed, she could only think of Frank, young, red-haired, grinning, full of stories, and the one story he swore was never a lie.

It was the fishing trip he'd had as a young lad. A humpback whale had tangled herself in a discarded net from another ship, and their little boat had found her upright in the water, straining for the surface. They thought she was dead until a gust of breath spurted from her blowhole, but she had no strength left. The nets were tangled so tightly around her fins that the water flushed red when they managed to release her. The whole process took over an hour, he told her, while the whale struggled to lift her head high enough to catch her breath.

But when they did set her free, the whale did not flee like they expected, but followed in the wake of their ship, breaching the surface and collapsing back under the waves as if she were dancing, throwing herself between sea and sky with all the joy of having touched death and finding herself alive once more.

Catherine Stanford

As if by Magic
(novel extract)

Prologue
Wednesday 4th June 1913

The moment her head touches the ground, history
will be made. Of course, I don't know this yet and
neither do the rest of the crowd, swelling impatiently
under the midday sun. It is a fine Wednesday in
June and I'm sitting on the front step of the house,

fussing over a blouse. Miles away in Surrey, the King and Queen look out onto the course from the Royal Box. Perhaps the King is nervous, twitching impatiently at his gloves as he wonders where his colt will place. Perhaps the Queen sips lemonade indifferently or glances anxiously at her husband from under the brim of her hat.

While I thread my needle the leaders thunder around Tattenham Corner. Craganour and Aboyeur lead the way, champing and biting at each other. Day Comet, Great Sport and Louvois all follow: flashes of silken grey and brown bolting down the green under the cloudless sky. I pull the thread taut. The horses flash past and flick turf into the faces of the crowd. Do the people cheer with excitement? Are they taken back to some childhood memory by the pungent smell in the air? Mother calls to me from the kitchen and I reply, the work drooping in my lap. This could be when it happened. Maybe, when my mother's voice rang out across the court yard, the idea first took flight.

A woman stands on Tattenham Corner. The woman is Emily Davison: a perfectly ordinary looking person, as ordinary as myself, with dark hair and a white blouse. She does not know that in the next five minutes she will sustain fatal injuries for which she will be remembered in years to come. She doesn't know that people will write articles about her, hoping to unravel the mysterious enigma of her death.

The leaders are on the home straight now. A wrong stitch causes a drop of blood to blossom on the fabric. The King dabs at his brow. Emily looks around frantically, breathlessly, as she grips the white rail (or is she calm and collected? Does she steady herself with deep breaths?)

I sigh and squint. The sun is unbearable. It glares through the smoggy clouds that obscure the sky line of the city. There is tension in the air and a prickling down my neck that tells me a storm is brewing.

Dare she do it? Can she persuade her shaking legs to move? She feels leaden, sinking into the ground. Time has stopped and the thundering hooves in the distance are the sounds of the world turning as my hands work the fabric.

I suck my finger and scowl at the ivory blouse, which is turning grey in the sooty air. It's too hot to sew today and I feel irritable, provoked, wishing that the clouds would break. The finish line is in sight. People shield their eyes from the sun with hands and parasols. Emily takes a deep breath — then she moves.

Nobody notices her, not at first. She totters out, stumbling over the divots that the horses have made and breathes unsteadily. At the last moment, she finds her feet. Already the horses are coming, quicker — so much quicker than she could have ever expected. She reaches out, not thinking it would have been like this, not realising quite how powerful they are until their muscular bulk is upon her and the air is knocked effortlessly from her lungs. Her body jerks, twists, jarred and strange like a mannequin with snapped strings. She hurtles across the ground. The camera is rolling; the horses whinny and buck. She falls. Her eyes roll, unfocused. The body makes impact, touches the ground and then skids to a halt. At last it is all over. Aboyeur wins the race. I tire of the heat and finally turn back into the house.

When I would look back at the article, years later, I'd always think that the photograph made her seem suspended in midair, levitating inches from the ground, as if by magic. Francis sometimes joked that he was the one doing it but I never cared for jokes about things like that.

She died four days later, Lord bless her. I didn't know that then. I reckon there was a lot I didn't know actually.

I was only 17, living in what would come to be known as the slums of Sheffield, a rundown back-to-back in Park Hill where four of us crammed into three tiny rooms. Whether I'm a true Yorkshire lass or not, I guess I'll never know. My real mother appeared from nowhere and was gone just as quickly. Even so I've always taken Sheffield to be home, regardless of my true origin. Although, with every passing day, it feels like I was born into a different world entirely. Lamplighters and corsets only exist in history books now; gone are the music halls and the stars that trod the boards. The horses no longer trot up Fargate and the farriers' fires have long gone cold.

It's a strange sensation to look into your past and feel as though you are viewing it through amber. Everything seems hazy, half preserved. Perhaps I've looked at one too many photographs over the years because sometimes the colour bleeds out of my memories and they become black and white too ... but the year before the first war, my life was a riot of colour and smell.

It was the shine of Francis' hair under the stage lights, parted down the middle and as polished as Whitby jet. It was the white and red of grease paint sticks; the working men coming straight to the halls from the factories, glistening with ebony sweat. It was bolts of purple and jade satin, imported from across the ocean and the smell

of pipe smoke, spices and spilled ale. It was the year
that I had my first kiss and the year that I got my first
proper job.

Yes, 1913 is a lifetime ago now. Before concrete
buildings and women in trousers and even before
I met Cornelius, I was just plain old Margaret Finnely;
but even the plainest of people can do remarkable
things. This is a story about family, friendship and
how you should never judge a book by its cover. And
most of all, it's a story about magic.

'It was her! I know it was!'

'Why would I bother with that? As if I haven't got
enough to do without making extra work for myself!'

Oh *bugger*. There wasn't much point in trying to
defend myself. I'd been sussed out already.

'Girls, just calm down please!'

The problem is, whenever I've done something
wrong, I have the overwhelming urge to laugh.
Like when somebody tells you something sad. You
know you should be upset that their granny has
finally popped her clogs or that their dog has died
but instead of making you sad it fills you up with the
desire to laugh, bubbling all the way up your throat
until you have to pretend that you just need to
yawn or sneeze. I suppose it sounds cruel but maybe
it's just because I never had a granny or a dog or
anything like that, so I don't care so much. I shove
my tongue into my bottom lip and ignore the burn of
mother's eyes on my cheek.

'You're a lying little trollop Margaret Finnely and
everybody knows it!' Cecily snarls.

She is glaring down at me, looking like she is
just about ready to pounce. I brace the step with my
hands. It wouldn't be the first time I've come a
cropper when trying to get one over on Cecily. We've

grown up together, her house being just along
from ours, so everyone supposes we should
be good chums but I can't stand the bitch. (That's
a word Francis taught me. I've heard it in quite a
few of the acts at the hall too but I don't dare say it
aloud, not if I don't want my block knocking off
anyway.)

'Eh! We'll have less of that if you don't mind!'
Mother steps in at last, drawing herself up to her full
height. Cecily backs away, steaming. I've had a
few shiners from Cecily before and I'd be glad not
to have another one if I can help it.

'Whether Maggie did it or not, I'm not having that
sort of language around here!' She turns to face
me now, her jowls trembling in spectacular fashion.
'And you!'

She's quite a good egg sometimes, mother is.
Not that she's my real mother. Even if they didn't
know already, the neighbours wouldn't have to
be bright sparks to know that the stork left me under
the wrong mulberry bush. She isn't even obliged
to stick up for me but she gives me a helping hand
whenever she can. I don't reckon it's even out of
kindness. I just think she feels bad for how small and
sickly looking I turned out, that's all.

'You fix this!' The beads of sweat on her upper
lip glint in the sun as she throws the ruined petticoat
at me. It whips my face before landing in my lap.
Cecily starts to laugh cattily but one glance from
mother's dark eyes and she quickly pipes down.
Mother sniffs and pushes past me into the kitchen.

Truth be told, Cecily scares me something
rotten. She's left me with more than my fair share of
bruises over the years, which is easy enough to
do considering she's twice the size of me. Once she
is satisfied that mother is out of ear shot, she gets

up close to me again and folds her arms over her vast bust. She smells of face powder and bacon fat.

'Not so smug now, are you?' Her smile is aggravatingly catty too, which is bizarre really because she looks much more like a piglet.

'Now then, what was it you've been calling me? Oh yes, that's it — Jam Roly-Poly. Well, I'd much rather be a Jam Roly-Poly than a skinny, unwanted little bastard like you!'

A door slamming somewhere on the street makes us both start but it's just Mr Jones, running for the privy again. We watch as he hobbles down the lane, clutching at his stomach as he goes. Lasses scrapping isn't an uncommon sight down this way.

'Nothing to say back to that? What a surprise. I don't know why they put up with a juggins like you. I'd be carting you off to the nut house if I had half a chance.'

A nasty sneer flits over her features and then she turns on her heel, swaying away like she's Lady bleeding Godiva. I flick my thumb up at her but only a little bit, just in case.

Fucking Cecily! (Another one I've picked up from the halls — a real London swear that one is!)

She likes nothing better than to get me riled up with a few choice words. At least they don't smart so much anymore. I've heard it all before. There isn't much point in pretending that I'm not a skinny little bastard, because I am. Francis tells me not to say it about myself but I don't care either way.

The weather is horrible again today, sticky and thick, just like yesterday. It's even worse down here because we're so close to the works that all the smog keeps the heat in like a big black blanket. The privy bloody reeks as well — I can hear Mr Jones groaning now. Everybody is waiting for the rain;

I'd happily put up with the leaking roof in the attic if it just meant I could cool down.

In the distance, the Cathedral bells are chiming. I listen closely and count. Eleven o'clock. That means Francis will be home soon.

There's nothing much wrong with the rag in my hand, just a split seam. It won't take more than a minute to fix. Besides, I wouldn't have done it at all if she hadn't have pinched me so hard. The bruise is still there on my arm, inky blue, looking queer among my red freckles. I won't show Francis though, he always gets so upset.

The heat of the kitchen is sweltering. Mother has the fire ready to make dinner. What with being so tall, she always looks out of place stood by the range. She has to stoop almost double just to get the coals going. At six-foot-four, she's intimidating for a bird and has more of a moustache than most blokes. Mother is dark all over. Dark thick eyebrows and large brown eyes, with skin like an Italian. Children always ask her if she is but she says it's just because she's been in the city for too long and the smog has got inside her, staining her from the inside out.

There is a certain way she holds herself when she is feeling mardy. She tenses her back and shoulders, bending her head close to her chest, pretending that she can't see us at all. She never keeps it up for long though. The muscles on her back ripple and quiver until finally she erupts with a question or another telling off.

I take my work basket down from the mantle and pull the stool away from the range. Normally that's where I'd take up my perch, stitching away by the light of the range. But it's too hot for that today and the soot will only make the petticoat even grottier.

Besides, I don't fancy getting all that close to mother, not while she's holding the paring knife.

Above my head, the floor boards creak. We share the house with Mrs Biggins who has the room above the kitchen, leaving us three to share the attic. Luckily for Francis, he is usually on the road and doesn't have to put up with mother's snoring and murmurings and the screams of Anne Marie next door when Mr Peterson comes in leery from the pub.

Mrs Biggins used to have the house next door when she had children. Six children in total and she outlived them all, to her greatest regret. Mr Biggins is long gone too, finished off when a cart overturned and crushed him. After all that, it seemed a bit unkind to leave her there by herself, without a penny to her name. I know mother would never have forgiven herself if she ended up in Fir Vale.

Despite her coughing and complaining, I don't mind having her here. Mrs Biggins is the only person who ever saw my real mother in the flesh; it sounds to me as though she was the only one who ever showed her a bit of kindness too. It makes giving her the tar medicine that bit more bearable, knowing that maybe the same wrinkled lips that purse at the spoon once kissed my real mother's cheek.

My mother now, or Mrs Finnely if I was being proper, is still riled. She grabs the big pan off the hook and slams it onto the range with a deafening clang.

'You're being awful quiet Mam.'

She snorts at that and grabs hold of a turnip.

'I should think I am — wouldn't want to be on the wrong side of one of your comments, would I?

Hate to think what you would call me ... Spotted
Dick, probably.'

She doesn't laugh but I have to chew my lip to
stop myself from spluttering. A few embers fall out
of the fire and blow across the hearth.

'What I don't understand,' she says, turning to the
table, 'is why you insist on winding her up! You've
a real cheek, you know that?'

'She's the one that starts it!' But even I can hear
how petulant I sound and my cheeks burn hard.
When will the storm come and take away this bloody
heat?

'You ought to know better by now. You're 17, a
grown woman.'

'I don't look like a grown woman.' The needle
freezes in my hand. I didn't mean to say it out loud
but it came out nevertheless. Upstairs, the boards
creak again and Mrs Biggins hacks out a cough.

'Is that what you're upset about? Is that what all
this name calling and pinching is about? Because
you don't look like Cecily yet?'

I keep staring down at the fabric. My cheeks feel
hotter than ever now.

'Because if that's it, you're daft! I never saw
any two women who looked the same...' She blinks
and adds, 'Well, not unless they was twins, of
course.'

Mother wasn't one to speak about beauty and
looks. She didn't bother with rouge and she
had never even sniffed a jar of cold cream. I told her
once that I needed some cornmeal to brush through
my hair, and she laughed like I'd said I wanted to
run away and join the circus.

At the time, I took it as it was. I never doubted her
for moment. She always seemed so strong to me,
the kind of strong where it doesn't matter what you

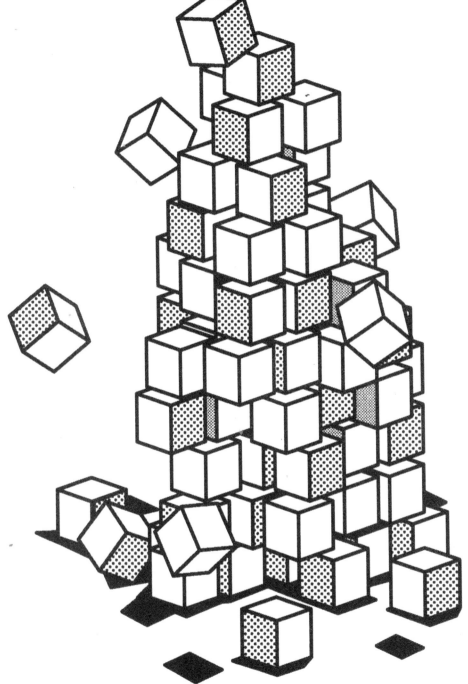

look like because nothing can ever break you.
I didn't think she even heard the little comments
when we were out and about, the whispers and
snide remarks, but that was just testimony to my
young naivety I suppose.

She is about to go on, her lined face taught with
worry when suddenly Francis appears from the lane,
battered and sleepy. He dumps his suitcase and
flashes us a tired but winning smile.

'Francis!'

I leap up at once, grateful for the opportunity
to bury my face in the collar of his jacket. He smells
wonderful and familiar, pipe smoke and grease
paint.

'Ayup, Magpie!' Francis is the only one who
stills calls me that. It's an old childhood nickname.
I grin into his neck and feel the press of his
sweaty skin against my cheek. He feels soft and
crumpled like a sleep worn blanket in the early
hours of the morning. After he kisses my cheek he
unceremoniously hands mother a bouquet of
travel-wilted carnations.

'Hello mam, you putting a brew on?' She's so
much taller than him that he has to crane up to kiss
her cheek. She takes the flowers and smells
them with delight, though there can hardly be any
perfume left in them at all.

'Hello love — good trip was it? You've caught the
sun I see. Pull up a chair for him, Maggie, that's
a good girl.'

I pull his chair out from the table at once and he
slumps into it, loosening his collar with two fingers.
There is a band of burnt red skin about his neck
but his face is the usual olive colour.

'It was alright ... nothing quite like home though
is there?'

Mother smiles at him and takes the kettle out
to go and fill it. Her eyes linger on me for a moment
but she shakes her head and decides whatever
she was going to say isn't worth saying. Or maybe
she doesn't want to embarrass me in front of
Francis.

I bring the stool up to his feet and pat my lap.
It doesn't much matter whether my dress gets dirty;
it's all old rags, anyway. Some folk would think
it was weird, me rubbing his feet like that and being
his sister. But sometimes, Francis is the only
person in the whole world who understands me.
We've never been apart. We might not be blood but
we're as good as.

'What do you know then Mag, anything good?'
My fingers are nimble and quick like always over his
laces, even though he makes a right job of knotting
them.

'Not much,' I shrug. 'It's been quiet with you gone.'
I don't fancy telling him about the Cecily incident
so instead I look up at him to see what he is thinking,
easing the soft leather over his heel. He is staring
at the range with a detached dreamy expression.
That's how he gets after a long journey. It's the
trains that do it I think. He gets so used to the world
rolling by, fields and cattle and rivers and such,
that it takes him a while to adjust back to things how
they are. Here in the house everything is nice and
still, just the embers scuttling across the hearth and
the clock ticking.

'Was it nice where you've just been? Was it the
seaside again?'

'Brighton? Course it's the seaside, you ninny!'
He grins. 'I'm going to take you and our mam there
next summer when I've got some more money
saved up. The crowd was a riot. Birds were all good

sports as well.' I slap him on the calf but smile too. He's only joking.

I don't think Francis is much for ladies really. I never saw him so much as peck a girl up here — and that's saying something because I know for a fact that Annie Phillips will go with a lad for two farthings round the side of The Albert if you ask her. In the pub he spins a real web, telling everybody that the girls down South are real goers but the truth is I think he couldn't tell if he wanted to. Maybe I should let him know about Annie Phillips.

'How long you staying for?'

'Oh, a month or what have you. Not got any other plans yet, I'll do a few spots up here.'

Some turns would be worrying if they weren't booked solid until December but not our Francis. He's got a charmed life. The act never gets old, you see, not like other magicians who all get found out sooner or later. What Francis does is real magic. That's what keeps them coming back, toffs and regular folk alike, the mystery of it. Sometimes in life, things happen and you can't explain how. Sometimes people are given gifts that you can't explain either. The story of how Francis got his gift is all to do with family and it's a story that I have to tell you if you want to really understand what sort of a person Francis is.

My real mother arrived in Sheffield in November 1896, when I was only a few weeks old. It was bitterly cold and there was already deep snow on the ground, although it wouldn't have been pearly white by any means. Snow in the city rarely was back then. She was dreadfully sick and couldn't get a boarding house to take her in, on account of her suspicious circumstances and terrible cough.

Without a farthing to her name, she wandered
around the streets, until at last she found herself in
Park Hill ... she must have desperate, poor love.
She was just about to lie down in the snow and give
it all up when Mrs Biggins came out to empty the
bed pan. At first she assumed it was just a bunch of
rags but then she heard a baby cry and realised it
was a person. One look at my mother's face sealed
the deal for her. She swore that my mother was
the spitting image of one of her own lost daughters,
so she couldn't have possibly left her outside.
I often wondered whether that bit was true. Mrs
Biggins often thought young women resembled
her daughters.

So she let her in the house and put her up in the
attic room. Mr Biggins was still alive then and said
that they could spare a bit of coal — a kind man,
he was — so they even lit a fire in the grate for her.
I was blue with cold, they said, and barely moving at
all. While my mother slept in the attic, they brought
me down to the kitchen and held me in front of
the range, giving me sips of gin to get the blood
flowing again. I like to think of it, even now. Old Mr
Biggins, rubbing my skin in front of the fire with
his large calloused hands until I bleated like a lamb
and woke from the cold at last.

Whilst I was gasping air into my tiny lungs, my
mother, unbeknownst to any of us, was taking
her last breath. When they went back upstairs to
check on her, she'd already died. They never
managed to find out her name or where she'd come
from. She didn't have a purse or a locket or anything.
The only thing she left behind, other than myself,
was a few spots of blood on the pillow by her mouth.

Mrs Biggins did the only thing she could think
of and cut off a lock of her hair, intending to keep it

for me if I grew up, so that I might at least have some small part of her.

This may not have a lot to do with Francis but I promise you, I'm getting there. While I was just starting out in life, Francis Finnely had already been around for three years. At that time, his father was still alive and the attic room was rented out by cousins. Even though the slums were just as dirty and poor as they are now, these were happy times for me. As soon as I was old enough, Francis and I spent nearly every day together. We played in the streets with the other children or went for long walks, hours from home, hoping to find ponds and lakes to collect tadpoles. An empty jar was hard to come by though, so we just had to look at them in our hands before we threw them back in.

He always made me laugh, even when we were hungry or cold, which was more often than not. Between Mr and Mrs Biggins and the Finnely's, I had a strange sort of extended family. If I had known my mother I'm sure I would have missed her, but I keep the locket of hair as a tribute to Mrs Biggins and her kindness more than anything else.

When Francis was seven and I was four, things changed suddenly. Mr Finnely did not come home from work one day. He was killed in an accident at the steel foundry. For a while, Francis was very quiet. He didn't come out to play much anymore. He spent a lot of time in his room doing ... well, I don't know what. Although I missed him, I was too young to understand and I still played out with the blissful ignorance that only children can have.

Then, about three months after that, Francis got his powers.

Hannah White

234

Route 57, Issue Eleven, The Feisty Font Revue
Full issue at www.route57.group.shef.ac.uk

General Editor	Adam Piette
Section Editors	Matthew Cheeseman
	Sam Ladkin
	Ágnes Lehóczky
	Carmen Levick
	Paula Morris

This volume edited by Matthew Cheeseman and Adam Piette
with Editorial Assistance from Camille Brouard, Kiran Dosanji
and William Watts.

Design	Go! Grafik, www.gografik.ch
Paper	Munken Print White 1.5
Typeface	Maax, Buster
Printing	New Goff, Ghent
Edition	500 copies

First published in the United Kingdom in 2015 by Feisty
Font Books, University of Sheffield and NATCECT
(www.einekleine.com/natcect).

This publication is generously funded by the University of
Sheffield's Faculty of Arts and Humanities Arts Enterprise fund.

The editors also gratefully acknowledge the support of Lyric
(www.sheffield.ac.uk/lyric), of Centre for Poetry and Poetics
(http://cppsheffield.tumblr.com), and the School of English
at the University of Sheffield (www.sheffield.ac.uk/english).

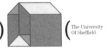